God's Word in *Your* Mouth

Changing Your World Through Faith

Jeff Doles

God's Word in Your Mouth:
Changing Your World Through Faith
© 2006 by Jeff Doles

Published by
Walking Barefoot Ministries
P.O. Box 1062, Seffner, FL 33583
www.walkingbarefoot.com

ISBN: 0-9744748-8-6

Contents

When It's All About God

*M*oses sent twelve men to spy out the land that was promised by God to the children of Israel. Ten came back and gave their report, which started out well but then suddenly turned dark:

> We went to the land where you sent us. It truly flows with milk and honey, and this is its fruit. Nevertheless the people who dwell in the land are strong; the cities are fortified and very large ... We are not able to go up against the people, for they are stronger than we ... The land through which we have gone as spies is a land that devours it inhabitants, and all the people whom we saw in it are men of great stature. There we saw the giants ... and we were like grasshoppers in our own sight, and so we were in their sight" (Numbers 13:27-28, 31-33).

The children of Israel — not a few, but the whole congregation — were exceedingly fearful when they heard this. They cried out against Moses and Aaron, and wished that they had never been brought out of Egypt in the first place, or else that they had perished along the way in the wilderness.

Only two spies came back with any good news, and they were bristling with confidence. One was Caleb, of the tribe of Judah. His name means "forcible." He tried to rally the people, firmly declaring,

"Let us go up at once and take possession, for we are well able to overcome it" (Numbers 13:30).

The other one was Hoshea, son of Nun, of the tribe of Ephraim. Moses called him Joshua, "The LORD is Salvation." When Joshua observed the great trepidation of the people and heard their venomous complaints, he and Caleb tore their garments and again tried to calm the fear, and awaken faith and courage in the people:

> The land we passed through to spy out is an exceedingly good land. If the LORD delights in us, then He will bring us into the land and give it to us, a land which flows with milk and honey. Only do not rebel against the LORD, nor fear the people of the land, for they are our bread; their protection has departed from them, and the LORD is with us. Do not fear them" (Numbers 14:7-9).

The congregation, however, would have none of it. "Stone them with stones," they cried.

Why was there such a huge difference between the report of Joshua and Caleb and that of the other ten spies? They all saw the same things. They were all working with the same set of facts. Yet, the ten looked at the situation and called it completely impossible, while Joshua and Caleb, seeing the exact same things, declared that victory was imminently doable.

The difference was in the orientation of their hearts. You see, there is no such thing as an uninterpreted fact. Though they all saw the same things, they looked at them in very different ways. They all had the same facts, but they perceived them from radically different perspectives, and it was the orientation of their hearts that determined their perceptions.

The difference in their orientations was in the difference of priority, of focus, and how they answered the question, Who is this all about? The ten spies looked at the situation as if it was all about them, their resources, their abilities, their strength. They looked in the natural and saw the people of Canaan as giants and themselves

6

as grasshoppers. They saw the natural world through natural eyes because that was the orientation of their hearts. They were leaning on their own understanding instead of trusting in the Lord with all their hearts (Proverbs 3:5).

The ten spies looked only with their natural eyes and then proceeded to say what they saw with those eyes, so they spoke out of a heart that thought this was all about them. "*We* are not able to go up against the people, for they are stronger than *we*." They saw the problem (giants in the land) and they saw themselves as grasshoppers, totally unequal to the challenge.

Contrast that with Joshua and Caleb, who looked in the spirit and viewed the natural through spiritual eyes. What did they see? They saw God, and the people of Canaan looked like grasshoppers before Him. They saw the same facts that the other ten saw, only they understood the truth about what they were seeing—that this was about God. Then they spoke according to what they saw: "We are well able to overcome … The LORD is with us."

Now, understand that Joshua and Caleb didn't deny that there was a problem. In fact, they freely acknowledged it. But they were unmoved by it: "Do not fear these people—they are our bread, and they have no protection." The orientation of their hearts was toward God. They saw that they were well able to overcome the problem because God was with them.

When its all about God, there is nothing to fear. Moses understood this long before he sent out the spies. He learned it when God first called him to deliver the children of Israel from cruel oppression. Moses hesitated. "Who am I that I should go to Pharaoh, and that I should bring the children of Israel out of Egypt?," as if any of this was about him and his abilities. But God corrected his defective understanding. "I will certainly be with you" (Exodus 3:11-12). This was not about Moses, but about God, and would, therefore, certainly come to pass. That is why Moses was in no way dissuaded by the negative report of the ten spies. He agreed with the report of Joshua and Caleb because he knew as well as they that God would be with them.

But God now pressed Moses' understanding even further. When the congregation called for Joshua and Caleb to be stoned, the Bible says, "the Glory of the LORD appeared in the tabernacle of meeting before all the children of Israel" (Numbers 14:10). Of course, this was not a good thing for the ten spies and the congregation, for whom God was not the priority. But set that aside for a moment and listen to what the Lord had to say to Moses:

> How long will these people reject Me? And how long will they not believe Me, with all the signs which I have performed among them? I will strike them with the pestilence and disinherit them, and I will make of you a nation greater and mightier than they. (Numbers 14:11-12)

This was a test: How much did Moses really understand concerning who this was all about. "Shall I destroy these people and make of *you* a greater nation, Moses?" But Moses was far past thinking it was about him, or even wanting it to be about Him. He quickly answered the LORD:

> Then the Egyptians will hear it, for by *Your* might *You* brought these people up from among them, and they will tell it to the inhabitants of this land. They have heard that *You*, LORD, are among these people; that *You*, LORD, are seen face to face and *Your* cloud stands above them, and *You* go before them in a pillar of cloud by day and in a pillar of fire by night. Now if *You* kill these people as one man, then the nations which have heard of *Your* fame will speak, saying, "Because the LORD was not able to bring this people to the land which *He* swore to give them, therefore *He* killed them in the wilderness." (Numbers 14:13-16, emphasis added).

Moses passed the test. His spiritual vision was 20/20. He knew exactly who this was all about—the Lord God of Israel. God's name,

God's power, God's glory, God's people. Then Moses appealed to God's mercy and asked Him to pardon the iniquity of the people for thinking it was about them. The Lord answered,

> I have pardoned, according to your word; but truly, as I live, all the earth shall be filled with the glory of the LORD—because all these men who have seen My glory and the signs which I did in Egypt and in the wilderness, and have put Me to the test now these ten times, and have not heeded My voice, they certainly shall not see the land of which I swore to their fathers, nor shall any of those who rejected Me see it. (Numbers 14:20-23)

Then of Caleb, whose heart was toward the Lord, He said,

> But My servant Caleb, because he has a different spirit in him and has followed Me fully, I will bring into the land where he went, and his descendants shall inherit it (v. 24).

Then the Lord had Moses deliver this message to the congregation:

> Just as you have spoken in My hearing, so I will do to you; The carcasses of you who have complained against Me shall fall in this wilderness, all of you who were numbered, according to your entire number, from twenty years old and above. Except for Caleb the son of Jephunnah and Joshua the son of Nun, you shall by no means enter the land which I swore I would make you dwell in. (vv. 28-30)

Notice that everyone received *exactly* what they had spoken: The congregation said, "Better we should die in the wilderness." And so they did. The ten spies said, "We are not able to go up against the people of Canaan." And so they never did go up against them, but died of a plague in the wilderness. Joshua and Caleb said, "We are well able to overcome ... The LORD is with us." And in time they entered and took possession of the Promised Land (read about it in the book of Joshua).

They each got what they expected. They each experienced what they focused on. They each received according to *how* they saw, whether in the natural or in the Spirit. And they each obtained whatever they spoke, whether it was a good report or an evil report.

Who is this life all about? Those who think it is all about themselves walk in fear of every problem and situation that is bigger than them, and they will perish in the wilderness. Those who know it is all about God walk in faith, knowing that God is much bigger than any and every problem. They go on to enjoy victory in the Promised Land.

When you encounter giants in your life, problems that seem like they are much bigger than you, remember that it is no longer about you but about God. Take these steps:

▶ Stop focusing your attention on the problems and your ability to solve them.

▶ Start focusing your attention on the Lord. Get to know Him more and more, giving yourself completely to Him in prayer, praise and worship.

▶ Study the Word of God, searching out all His blessings, benefits and promises that pertain to your problem or need.

▶ As you discover these blessings and promises, start speaking what you see in the Word of God. His Word is true and cannot fail.

▶ Go forth and dwell in the Promised Land, because it's all about God.

God Will Deliver Us,
Without a Doubt!

*M*ost Christians have heard about Shadrach, Meshach and Abed-Nego—the three young Hebrew men who were delivered out of the fiery furnace. Those were the Babylonian names given to Hananiah, Mishael and Azariah, when they were carried off into exile and trained for service in the courts of the Babylonian king, Nebuchadnezzar (Daniel 1:7).

Now, Nebuchadnezzar made an image of gold to honor himself, and he decreed that, at a certain time, when all the instruments sounded, everyone should fall down and worship before it. Whoever failed to do so would be cast into the midst of a burning fiery furnace. The day came, the instruments sounded, and everyone fell down and worshiped the golden image—everyone except Shadrach, Meshach and Abed-Nego.

When it came to the king's attention that there were three young Hebrews who would not bow, he became enraged and had them brought before him. He gave them one last chance and said, "If you do not worship, you shall be cast immediately into the midst of a burning fiery furnace. And who is the god who will deliver you from my hands?" (Daniel 3:15).

Shadrach, Meshach, and Abed-Nego did not even try to defend themselves. They simply said, "O Nebuchadnezzar, we have no need to answer you in this matter. If that is the case, our God whom we serve is able to deliver us from the burning fiery furnace, and He will deliver us from your hand, O king. But if not, let it be known to you, O king, that we do not serve your gods, nor will we worship the gold image which you have set up" (Daniel 3:16-18 NKJV).

Getting the Story Right

Most Christians have heard this story, but many have misread it. They think it goes something like this: The three Hebrews answer Nebuchadnezzar and say, "O king, our God is able to deliver us, and He will deliver us. *But if he doesn't,* we still will not worship your image." According to this version, they were not sure that God would deliver them, and so they had a back-up answer in case God didn't come through on their behalf.

Some translations of the Bible even seem to support this reading. The NASB says, "He will deliver us out of your hand, O King. But *even* if *He does* not . . . we are not going to serve your gods." Notice the italicized words—they do not translate anything in the original Hebrew text, but were added by the translators in an attempt to bring clarity. But they actually do just the opposite. They distort the faith of Shadrach, Meshach and Abed-Nego. The NIV gives the same reading without even alerting the reader to the additional words by italicizing them.

Many other versions leave the original reading intact. For example, the King James Version, New King James Version, New Revised Standard Version, Revised English Bible, and the Amplified Bible all follow the Hebrew text without any additions. They simply say, "But if not ..."

But if not—what? This clause does not refer back to the statement "He will deliver us from your hand, O king," as if to say, "Maybe God will deliver us, or maybe God won't." No, not at all.

Rather, "but if not," in verse 18, relates back to the previous "if that is the case," in verse 17.

Nebuchadnezzar had just said that if the Hebrews did not bow, he would throw them into the fiery furnace. Then he asked, "And who is the god who will deliver you from my hands."

Here is the force of how the Hebrews answered: If that is the case, O king, and you throw us into the fiery furnace, then know this—our God is able to deliver us, and He will, in fact, deliver us. But if you do not throw us into the fiery furnace, then know this— we still will not worship your image or your gods.

A Clear Challenge

The three Hebrews not only believed that God *could* deliver them, but they were also confident that God *would* deliver them. There was no doubt in their words. They did not waver about it one bit.

There are two strong reasons why we know this. First, there is the relationship between the "if" and "if not" clauses. They correspond to each other, like bookends. They lay out the two options the king had before him—to throw the Hebrews in the furnace or not throw them in—and what the results would be in either event.

But there is no such textual reason to suppose that "but if not" refers to whether God would or would not deliver them. That has been nothing more than conjecture on the part of those who do not have a clear understanding about the difference between faith and doubt. "If" and "if not" are about Nebuchadnezzar's action, not God's.

Second, if the Hebrews thought that God might not deliver them, it would have been completely unnecessary for them to tell the king, in that event, that they would not worship his gods. That would have been self-evident. Imagine how silly it would have been for them to say: "If you throw us into the fiery furnace, and God does not deliver us, we will not bow down to your image." Of course they would not bow down—they would be dead. Burnt to a crisp. Vaporized! Dead men don't bow down to anything. So it would be quite pointless to for them to say what some have supposed them to have said.

What they actually said to the king was not pointless at all, but quite powerful: Pitch us in the furnace, O king. Our God will deliver us and we will continue to worship Him. And if you don't pitch us in the furnace, we are still going to worship our God and not yours. It was a strong challenge they were making to Nebu-chadnezzar. It was faith through and through, without any hint of doubt. They said what they believed—"God will deliver us"—and they received exactly what they said.

Faith is Not Double-Minded

The reason so many Christians misunderstand this story is that they do not understand faith and how it operates. They think it is somehow faith to say, "God will deliver us, but if He doesn't ..." as they suppose these young Hebrew men to have said. They think you can mix faith with doubt and still get results. The Bible calls that wishy-washy: "But let him ask in faith, with no doubting, for he who doubts is like a wave of the sea driven and tossed by the wind. For let not that man suppose that he will receive anything from the Lord; he is a double-minded man, unstable in all his ways"(James 1:6-8).

If the three Hebrews had said, "Maybe God will; maybe God won't" they would have had no reason to expect anything at all from the Lord. They would have been double-minded, unstable in all their ways—certainly not the faith heroes who "quenched the violence of fire" (Hebrews 11:34). It is faith that pleases God, not doubt (Hebrews 11:6).

Other Christians have problems believing that God is still in the miracle business, that we can trust Him to deliver us in any situation, and expect to see it happen. So they rationalize the faith of these Hebrew champions to give God (and themselves) an escape clause.

They often do the same thing when they add "if it be Thy will" to their prayers. They either do not know the will of God, because they have not read His Word sufficiently, or else they do not really believe His promises. They don't really know if they will receive what they are asking, or what God has said, so they tack on "if it be Thy will." That way, they are covered no matter what happens.

That is not faith, but doubt. It is double-mindedness and instability. They think God is wishy-washy because they are wishy-washy, and there is nothing God-pleasing in that.

Activated Faith

Shadrach, Meshach and Abed-Nego operated in faith because they knew God. They knew His name. They knew His ways. They knew His Word. They knew His heart. It is impossible to live by faith without knowing God. The Bible says, "But without faith it is impossible to please Him, for he who comes to God must believe that He is, and that He is a rewarder of those who diligently seek Him" (Hebrews 11:6). The man or woman of faith does not add, "But if He doesn't ..."

If you need more faith, get to know God more. Get into His Word and you will begin to discover His will and His ways. "Faith comes by hearing, and hearing by the Word of God" (Romans 10:17). As you listen to the Word of God, and receive the words of His heart into your heart, faith will begin to stir inside you.

It is not enough to simply *have* faith, however. You must know how to use it. Faith is not just a noun, it is also a verb. It is alive and active.

Faith is activated, or exercised, by what we say. Jesus said, "For assuredly, I say to you, whoever says to this mountain, 'Be removed and be cast into the sea,' and does not doubt in his heart, but believes that those things he says will be done, he will have whatever he says" (Mark 11:23).

The three Hebrews said what they believed: "God will deliver us." They did not mix any doubt with that. They did not allow themselves any escape clause. They believed what they said, said what they believed and received what they said.

That is how faith works. We believe what God has said, then say the same thing. God is honored by that, and is not pleased even one tiny bit without it. He honors His word in our mouths just as much as He honors it in His own mouth.

The principle really is simple: Believe God in your heart. Do not doubt. Say what you believe. If you will learn to do that, you will begin to walk in the realm of authority that Shadrach, Meshach and Abed-Nego learned to walk in.

And God will deliver you—without a doubt!

Seven Things Working Together
for Your Good

*And we know that all things work together for good
to those who love God, to those who are the
called according to His purpose.
(Romans 8:28)*

This is a favorite Bible passage for many Christians. The common understanding of this verse has generally been that all things, whether they be good, bad or indifferent, work together in the plan of God to bring about good for those who love Him.

This view is something of a sacred cow, but it needs to be challenged because it has brought about a dangerous misunderstanding of the means and purposes of God. It confuses goodness with that which is actually the enemy of goodness. When it is followed to its logical conclusion, it tends to make God the creator of evil.

In this view, when something bad happens, we are obliged to paint it as somehow contributing to the good rather than stealing from it. The result is that we often tend to accept the bad instead of standing against it with the promises of God. We may even end up stepping away from what God has promised, all because we have missed what this passage is really talking about.

Yes, there are some Bible translations that render this text as,

"And we know that God causes all things to work together for good" (NASB), making God the subject of this verse. But that is not found in the majority of the Bible manuscripts or lectionary readings in the early Church. The majority of texts have "all things" as the subject. In other words, this verse is not about what God does in all things, but about "all things" themselves working together for good.

There are a couple of observations to make here: First, the word "things" ("all *things* work together") is not necessary to the translation. We may just as well simply say, "all work together for good." Nor is it necessary to take "all things" in an absolute sense, that is, as referring to everything that has ever existed or happened, whether good or bad. We may understand "all" to refer simply to those things which are particularly mentioned within the context of Romans 8. Notice also that the "working together" of all things is cast in the present tense. That is, all these things are presently working together for our good. They are available and active right now on behalf of those who love the Lord.

We do not have to tolerate, accept, bless or be thankful for any of the bad or evil things that happen in our lives, as if they are somehow necessary for our good (they are not), or that they somehow add to the quality of our lives (they do not).

Now, certainly God can take a bad situation and bring good out of it. After all, isn't that what our redemption is all about, God buying back and setting free that which has come under the power of evil? But that is not at all the same thing as evil somehow working together to bring about good.

And certainly God can teach us in the midst of whatever evil things may happen to us. But that does not in any way make evil our teacher, nor should we think of it that way. God has given us the Holy Spirit as our teacher (John 14:26; 1 John 2:20, 27), and He does not need to use evil to teach us anything.

Evil is about bringing forth evil, not about bringing forth good. Even if evil could work together with good, the final result would not be good, but a diminished good. Evil is the lack of good, so that even a little lack of good, as in a mixture of good and evil, is still a lack of good, and therefore ultimately evil.

But no, that is not God's way. God is completely good, and He does not cooperate with evil to bring about good. Rather, He works to deliver that which is good from that which is evil. God's way is to overcome evil with good (Romans 12:21).

So, if the "all" of Romans 8:28 is not about evil things and good things working together to bring about the good, then what is it about? In this case, "all" is speaking about the same things that Paul has just finished discussing earlier in Romans 8. All these things not only work together for good, but they are all, in themselves, good. Paul's point is that, though there may be many things trying to work against us for evil, there are also many other, greater things working together for our good.

Before we consider these things, notice the words "work together" in verse 28. The underlying Greek word is *sunenergeo*. It is a compound made up of the word *sun*, "together," and *energeo*, which is where we get the word "energy." *Sunenergeo* is the expending of energy in a cooperative effort to produce a desired result. In Romans 8, there are a number of other words with the prefix *sun* and its alternate forms, *sum*, *sus*, and *sug*, all indicating things which are now operating together. These are brought out in the following list.

1. The Law of the Spirit of Life

"For the law of the Spirit of life in Christ Jesus has made us free from the law of sin and death" (Romans 8:2). Notice that the law of the Spirit of life does not cooperate, or work together with, the law of sin and death. Rather, it sets us free from it.

2. The Spirit of Adoption

"For you did not receive the spirit of bondage again to fear, but you received the Spirit of adoption by whom we cry out 'Abba, Father'" (Romans 8:15). Notice, again, that the Spirit of adoption does not cooperate with the "spirit of bondage again to fear," but acts in opposition to it.

Then Paul adds, "The Spirit bears witness with our spirit that we are children of God" (v. 16). The phrase "bears witness with" is the Greek *summartureo*. That is, they work together to bear witness.

Paul continues, "and if children, then heirs—heirs of God and joint-heirs with Christ, if indeed we suffer with Him, that we may also be glorified together" (v. 17). Here, in one brief sentence, are three instances of the Greek prefix meaning "together." We are "joint-heirs," (*sugkleronomos*), or heirs together with Christ. If we suffer together (*sumpascho*) with Him, we will also be glorified together (*sundoxazo*) with Him.

3. The Earnest Expectation of Creation

For the earnest expectation of the creation eagerly waits for the revealing of the sons of God. For the creation was subjected to futility, not willingly, but because of Him who subjected it in hope; because the creation itself also will be delivered from the bondage of corruption into the glorious liberty of the children of God. For we know that the whole creation groans and labors with birth pangs together until now. (Romans 8:19-22)

When Adam and Eve sinned, the whole creation fell under the curse and suffered with them. The Greek indicates that the whole creation "groans together" (*sustenazo*), as well as experiences travail together (*sunodino*). Creation waits to experience together with us the glorious liberty of the children of God.

When God created the heavens and the earth, and everything in them, He pronounced them "good" (see Genesis 1, throughout).

Though they have been subject to the Fall, there are laws still present within creation for bringing about the good. For example, the principle of seedtime and harvest (that is, sowing and reaping) is in effect as long as the earth remains (Genesis 8:22). This means that if we sow evil, we will reap evil, but it we sow good, we will reap good (see also Galatians 6:7-8).

4. The Firstfruits of the Spirit

Not only that, but we also who have the firstfruits of the Spirit, even we ourselves groan within ourselves, eagerly waiting for the adoption, the redemption of our body. (Romans 8:23).

Just as creation groans and travails together to bring forth good, we also groan within ourselves, anticipating the adoption—the redemption of our bodies from corruption. We groan together with creation, and creation groans together with us.

We have already received the firstfruits of this adoption—the Holy Spirit, who is the promise of the Father to the Church at Pentecost, the "Feast of Firstfruits." We now have all the fruits of the Spirit as well as the gifts of the Spirit at work in us and on our behalf.

5. Hope

"For we were saved in this hope, but hope that is seen is not hope; for why does one still hope for what he sees?" (Romans 8:24) The Greek word for "hope" is *elpis*, and refers to a positive expectation, a joyful anticipation. Because it is oriented toward the future, it helps us stay on track in the present. We have a hope, a joyful expectation rooted in the promise of God, the work of Christ, and the indwelling of the Holy Spirit. As Paul said in Romans 5:5, "Hope does not disappoint." Our anticipation of good will be fulfilled, just as God promised.

6. Patience

"But if we hope for what we do not see, we eagerly wait for it with perseverance" (Romans 8:25). If we are oriented by hope, then we also need to have perseverance. The Greek word for "perseverance" is *hupomone*, and means "constancy, endurance, patience."

We know that faith and hope work together, for "faith is the substance of things hoped for" (Hebrews 11:1). Faith and patience also work together, for "the testing of your faith produces patience" (James 1:3). So, patience and hope work together also. We persevere because we believe, and expect to see God's plan fulfilled.

7. The Holy Spirit Helping Our Weakness

Likewise the Spirit also helps in our weaknesses. For we do not know what we should pray for as we ought, but the Spirit Himself makes intercession for us with groanings which cannot be uttered. Now He who searches the hearts knows what the mind of the Spirit is, because He makes intercessions for the saints according to the will of God. (Romans 8:26-27)

Notice, the Holy Spirit "helps" us. This is the Greek word *sunantilambanomai*, which speaks of two parties laying hold together, each one doing his part, to obtain a goal. The Holy Spirit does this by interceding for us with groanings which cannot be uttered, but which perfectly express the will of God for us. The whole creation groans, we groan within ourselves, the Holy Spirit groans within us—all working together to bring forth good.

Which brings us up to verse 28: "And we know that all work together for good to those who love God, to those who are the called according to His purpose."

From the context of Romans 8, we see that this is not about good working together with evil to produce good (which is logically impossible and morally suspect). No, this is about all the things Paul has already mentioned—the Spirit of life, the Spirit of adoption, the groaning of creation, the firstfruits of the Holy Spirit, hope, patience, and the Spirit Himself interceding for us—all of *these* are always working together for good to those who love God and are called according to His purpose.

We are hard-pressed to understand how all kinds of evil things can work together to bring about good. It just doesn't add up for us, and rightly so. On the other hand, it is very easy for us to understand how all the things Paul talks about in Romans 8 actually do work together to bring about our good. They have a specificity to them which we can lay hold of by faith, and they are more than adequate to deal with any adversity we might face.

Let us, therefore, turn loose of the vague, dark notion that all things, good and evil, somehow add up to complete good. Instead, let's lay hold of all the thoroughly good, God-ordained things Paul talks about in Romans 8, things which are working together to bring about our good and fulfill God's purpose.

Pulling Paul's "Thorn"
The All-Sufficiency of God's Grace

And lest I should be exalted above measure by the abundance of the revelations, a thorn in the flesh was given to me, a messenger of satan to buffet me, lest I be exalted above measure. Concerning this thing, I pleaded with the Lord three times that it might depart from me. And He said to me, "My grace is sufficient for you, for My strength is made perfect in weakness." (2 Corinthians 12:7-9)

There are many Christians who believe that God afflicts His people with health problems, and this is the prime verse they use to present that teaching. They are well-meaning and seek to offer encouragement to those who are sick, but there are some important things they have not understood about this text, and that is:

▸ The nature of Paul's "thorn"

▸ The nature of God's grace

▸ The nature of sufficiency

The Nature of Paul's "Thorn"

A common teaching says that God gave Paul a sickness to keep him from becoming proud. Today, this supposed sickness is often identified as a malady of the eyes, based on passages such as Galatians 4:13-15:

> You know that because of physical infirmity I preached the gospel to you at the first … I bear you witness that, if possible, you would have plucked out your own eyes and given them to me.

Historically, however, interpreters have differed widely over the identification of this thorn, even as to whether it was a sickness at all. Even those who decided it was a malady were divided about what sort it might have been.

Let's take a closer look. First, notice that Paul explicitly describes this "thorn" as a "messenger of *satan*." So, *whatever* this thorn may have been, we know that it came from satan. God did not afflict Paul to punish him, humble him or teach him a lesson. In fact, God did not give it to him at all. On the other hand, the devil had ample reason for wanting to bring Paul down and destroy the influence he had because of the many revelations he received from the Lord.

Second, Paul does not call this "thorn" a sickness. Rather, he specifically identifies it as "a *messenger* of satan." The underlying Greek word for "messenger" is *angellos* which, as you can probably guess, is where we get the word "angel." This word appears over180 times in the Bible, and in every instance, it refers to a personal being. Not once is it used to refer to a thing, much less to a sickness or disease.

Third, "thorn in the flesh" is nowhere else found in the Bible to be referring to sickness or disease. In Numbers 33:55, the Lord warned Israel, "If you do not drive out the inhabitants of the land from before you, then it shall be that those whom you let remain shall be irritants in your eyes and *thorns in your flesh*, and they shall harass you in the land where you dwell." Joshua reiterates, "They shall be snares and traps to you, and scourges on your sides and *thorns in your eyes*" (Joshua 23:13). In Judges 2:3, we read, "They shall be *thorns in your side*, and their gods shall be a snare to you."

The figure of "thorns in the flesh" is used only to refer to adversarial persons. Paul's "thorn in the flesh," which he identified as a "messenger of satan," most likely referred to demonically influenced persecutors. This should come as no surprise, for Jesus promised that there would be persecutions (Mark 10:30), and Peter warned that our adversary the devil is prowling around like a roaring lion, seeking someone to devour (1 Peter 5:8).

Paul does speak about infirmities (weaknesses) in 2 Corinthians 12:10, along with the reproaches, needs, persecutions, and distresses he endured for Christ's sake. However, these were not identified as sicknesses, but as attacks from the enemy.

The Nature of God's Grace

Though Paul pleaded with the Lord three times that this thorn in the flesh might depart from him, God answered, "My grace is sufficient for you, for My strength is made perfect in weakness."

Many preachers and teachers have treated the grace of God in this passage as little more than a kindly disposition. It is a coping mechanism to help you learn how to live with the problem, to bear up pleasantly under it while the messenger of satan is beating you about your head and shoulders. It is portrayed as victory, but it looks very much like defeat. This kind of "grace" does little to solve the problem

But the grace of God is much more than a simple, kindly disposition of God toward us. It is not an idle wish for our well-being, not a coping mechanism, not a divine apathy that allows you to acquiesce to the abuse of the enemy. That would not even begin to be sufficient for anybody. No, the grace of God is backed with all the power and force of heaven—the divine power that created the universe. Grace is God's readiness to move heaven and earth on your behalf. It is a divine empowerment that enables you to defeat the enemy altogether.

The Nature of Sufficiency

God said, "My grace is sufficient for you." His grace is enough to meet the need. In fact, it is more than enough. Paul spoke earlier in this epistle about the grace of God and its sufficiency to meet every need:

> And God is able to make all grace abound toward you, that you always having all sufficiency in all things, may have an abundance for every good work. (2 Corinthians 9:8)

Abundance is having every need fully met with plenty extra. It is more than enough. When God says that His grace is sufficient, He does not mean that it will help you learn to live with lack and muddle through defeat. No, His grace is much greater than that. It comes to meet every need, solve every problem and enable you to live in victory—with plenty of resources left over to bless others.

The real problem was that Paul was trying to get God to do something He had already done, to grant something He had already provided. Paul already had the divine ability and authority of God to deal with this satanic messenger, and it was more than enough to defeat the enemy. Paul learned how to draw on that divine ability, which is why he could boldly declare,

> Therefore most gladly I will rather boast in my infirmities, that the power of Christ may rest upon me ... for when I am weak, then I am strong. (2 Corinthians 12:9-10)

This problem was no longer about Paul and his own strength, but about the mighty power and purpose of God. The Bible says, "For this purpose the Son of God was manifest, that He might destroy the works of the devil" (1 John 3:8). This same power of Christ was upon Paul to destroy the messenger of satan.

Yes, the devil has a plan for you, to derail and destroy you. He sends his messengers to inflict you with thorns. But Paul said, "We are not ignorant of his devices" (2 Corinthians 2:11), and you don't have to put up with his tactics.

God has a bigger plan for you, and His grace is overwhelming in its abundance. It does not come to teach you how to live with the problem. It comes to obliterate the problem, meet every need, and totally destroy every work of the devil in your life. God has given you mighty armor so that you can stand against the devil's wiles (Ephesians 6:11). He has given you the shield of faith to quench all the fiery darts of the wicked one (Ephesians 6:16). The grace of God is more than sufficient for you so that you can walk in His abundance and victory.

Framed by the Word

The Bible teaches us that faith is the substance, or the underlying reality, of the things we are expecting to see. Faith is the evidence, or proof, of things which cannot be seen. It exposes, or brings to light, things which cannot be perceived with our physical senses, and causes us to understand things which are not visibly manifest (Hebrews 11:1).

This is important because, as the author of Hebrews points out, it is by faith that men and women of old obtained a good report (Hebrews 11:2). That is, God was pleased with them because of their faith. We see this in Genesis, for example, when Abraham believed God and it was accounted to him for righteousness (Genesis 15:6). In other words, faith is how we are brought into "rightness" with God.

The remainder of Hebrews 11 shows how faith played out in the history of the Old Testament saints. But let's focus on verse three, which speaks of faith and the foundation of physical reality.

> By faith we understand that the worlds were framed by the Word of God, so that the things which are seen were not made of things which are visible. (Hebrews 11:3)

By Faith We Understand

Notice the order of this statement: By faith we understand. This has something very important to say, about both faith and understanding. First, faith does not come by understanding. We do not gather up all our empirical data, apply all our powers of reasoning and, by formulating theories or developing persuasive arguments, arrive at the doorstep of faith.

We do not reason our way to faith; we receive it by revelation. The Bible says that faith comes by hearing, and hearing by the Word of God (Romans 10:17). Faith is not a product of the mind, it is a gift of God that arises in our spirit whenever the Word of God is acutely presented to us by His Spirit.

Second, understanding comes by faith. In the world, we are taught that understanding is the product of reflecting on the input of the physical senses, or that it arises out of the interplay between the mind, the emotions and the natural world. That may be true in some ways, but only superficially so, for it does not penetrate to the heart of reality.

The Bible says that understanding comes by faith. Faith works on a different plane than does our understanding, and brings forth higher things than those which originate in the human heart.

"For My thoughts are not your thoughts,
    Nor are your ways My ways," says the LORD.
"For as the heavens are higher than the earth,
    So are My ways higher than your ways,
And My thoughts than your thoughts."

(Isaiah 55:8-9)

Though God's ways and thoughts are other and higher than our own, He is more than willing to share them with us and bring us up into them. He reveals them to us by His Word. Faith comes by hearing the Word, and understanding comes by faith.

That is why the Bible says, "Trust in the Lᴏʀᴅ with all your heart, and lean not on your own understanding. In all your ways acknowledge Him, and He shall direct your paths" (Proverbs 3:5-6). When we trust in the Lord, leaning fully on Him instead of on our own understanding, He gives us a *new* understanding, one that seeks after *His* thoughts and follows in *His* ways.

The Worlds Were Made by the Word of God

By faith, we understand something very important about the structure of reality: The worlds were framed and brought to completion by the Word of God. The heavens and the earth did not always exist. They had a beginning: God spoke.

We see this in Genesis 1. God said, "Let there be light," and there was light. He said, "Let there be a firmament," and so there was. "Let the waters be gathered," He said, and they were. "Let the earth bring forth," "Let there be lights in the firmament," "Let the waters abound with abundance of teeming creatures." All these things happened because God spoke them.

Then God said, "Let us make man in our image." And so He did. Our very existence is dependent upon the Word of God. No wonder the Scriptures record, "Man shall not live by bread alone, but by every Word that proceeds from the mouth of God" (Deuteronomy 8:3, Matthew 4:4).

The physical reality of this world is created and shaped by the Word of God, for He is a speaking God, and we are speaking creatures, created in His image to exercise dominion over His creation. That is why Adam was given the assignment of naming the animals (Genesis 2:19-20). Their identities and destinies were infused into them by their names, and Adam was the one who spoke these names over them. By his words, Adam acted on God's behalf, and the reality of the natural world was shaped.

Jesus spoke words to the wind and the waves, and there was

peace and stillness. He spoke words to the fig tree, and it withered and died. He taught the disciples to speak words to the mountains of difficulty they would encounter. He promised that, when the words of their mouths were matched by faith in their hearts, their words would be fulfilled and they would receive what they said (Mark 11:23).

Words are important. They are the basis of reality. Jesus said, "The words that I speak to you are spirit, and they are life" (John 6:63). Our lives are not founded on the natural realm, but on the spiritual—on every Word that proceeds from the mouth of God, imparted to us by His Spirit.

Things Which are Seen are Not Made of Things Which are Visible

The world teaches us to walk by sight and to understand according to what is seen. The Bible teaches us to "walk by faith, not by sight" (2 Corinthians 5:7), for those things which are seen are not made of things which are visible.

When we walk by sight, our understanding is dependent upon information that is superficial and will always be found wanting. But when we walk by faith, depending upon the Word of God, we penetrate to the heart of reality, which is framed by that very Word. Then we have an understanding that is based on a firm foundation.

We see this exampled in the life of Abraham (see Romans 4:16-22). God spoke a word to him: "I have made you a father of many nations" (v.17). In the natural, this made no sense at all, for both Abraham and Sarah, who had been barren all their lives, were now well past child-bearing years. If Abraham had walked by sight, he would have had no hope. But Abraham walked by faith and believed God, "who gives life to the dead and calls those things which do not exist as though they did" (v.17).

And not being weak in faith, he did not consider his own body, already dead (since he was about a hundred years old), and the deadness of Sarah's womb. He did not waver at the promise of God through unbelief, but was strengthened in faith, giving glory to God, and being fully convinced that what He had promised, He was also able to perform. (Romans 4:19-21)

Abraham understood that the things which are seen are not founded upon things which are visible. So he paid no attention to the barrenness he and Sarah had experienced in the natural. He focused instead on the promise of God, even though he could not see it with his eyes. The word God spoke became more real to him than what he experienced with his senses or understood with his own thoughts. The result is that he became the father of many nations, "according to what was spoken" (v. 18).

The invisible is the foundation of the visible. The spiritual is the foundation of the natural. Spiritual words are the underlying reality of the physical realm, and the whole world is grounded in the Word of God.

Someone has said that, when you can see the invisible, you can do the impossible. This echoes the words of Jesus: "If you can believe, all things are possible to him who believes" (Mark 9:23). With the eyes of faith, Abraham saw the invisible and received the impossible, for things which are seen are not made of things which are visible.

Faith is being convinced about what we do not yet see. Faith causes us to perceive in our spirit what we cannot comprehend by our senses. By faith, we lay hold of the promises of God, who calls those things that are not as though they were. By faith, we perceive that the world is founded upon words—the Word of God. By faith, we see the invisible and receive the impossible. By faith, we speak to mountains, and they move. By faith, we understand, and change the world.

The Order of Reality

The Bible teaches us that "In the beginning, God created the heavens and the earth" (Genesis 1:1). Right from the start we learn that there are two dimensions to reality—one is spiritual, the other is physical, or natural. The greater of these realities is spiritual. For God, who created the physical world, is Spirit (John 4:24). The Creator is greater than that which is created, therefore, the spiritual dimension is greater than the physical.

We see that the heavens and the earth were created, and therefore had a beginning. But the spiritual realm has always existed, for God, who is Spirit, is eternal. Although there are created beings in the spiritual realm, such as angels, God Himself has always existed.

This means, for one thing, that the spiritual dimension does not depend upon the physical dimension. The physical realm is dependant upon the spiritual, for physical reality comes forth from spiritual reality.

Paul declared the all-encompassing nature of this dependence when he preached to the philosophers on Mars Hill:

> God, who made the world and everything in it, since He is Lord of heaven and earth, does not dwell in temples made with hands. Nor is He worshiped with men's hands, as though He needed anything, since He gives to all life, breath, and all things. And He has

made from one blood every nation of men to dwell on all the face of the earth, and has determined their pre-appointed times and the boundaries of their dwellings, so that they should seek the Lord, in the hope that they might grope for Him and find Him, though He is not far from each one of us; for in Him we live and move and have our being. (Acts 17:24-28)

Not only our life and all our activity, but our very existence depends upon God. What we know as physical reality is entirely dependent upon spiritual reality—the realm of God.

The Word of God

Now, let's observe how God brought physical reality into being. The Bible says, "By faith we understand that the worlds were framed by the word of God, so that the things which are seen were not made of things which are visible" (Hebrews 11:3).

God framed the world by His words. Here's how it happened. God said, "Let there be light," and there was light (Genesis 1:3). He said, "Let there be firmament," and there was firmament (v. 6). "Let the waters be gathered and let dry land appear," and it was so (v. 9). And so on, through six days of creation.

So we discover that the Word of God is a reality far greater than the created, physical reality we observe with our senses. For by His Word, God "calls those things which do not exist as though they did"(Romans 4:17). The prophet Isaiah understood that the Word of God accomplishes whatever He desires to do in the world:

For as the rain comes down,
    and the snow from heaven,
And do not return there,
    but water the earth,
    and make it bring forth and bud,
That it may give seed to the sower
    and bread to the eater,

So shall My word be that goes forth from My mouth;
    it shall not return to Me void,
But it shall accomplish what I please,
    and it shall prosper in the thing for which I sent it.

(Isaiah 55:10-11)

The Order of Reality

Back up a few verses, and you will discover why this is so:

"For My thoughts are not your thoughts,
    Nor are your ways My ways," says the LORD.
"For as the heavens are higher than the earth,
    So are My ways higher than your ways,
  And My thoughts than your thoughts"

(Isaiah 55:8-9)

The ways of the spiritual realm are higher than the ways of the physical world. The workings of heaven are higher than the workings of earth. The thoughts of God are higher than the thoughts of man.

This is the language of hierarchy. The things of God are of a greater order than the things of the natural man—that is, of those who live according to the natural realm).

If this is so, then what do the things of God—His ways and thoughts—have to do with you and me? The answer is that, although we have physical bodies and inhabit the natural realm, we are essentially spiritual beings. For God said, "Let Us make man in Our image, according to Our likeness," and God created man in His own image (Genesis 1:26-27; notice again how God spoke the word, and it was done).

The account of creation in Genesis 2 expands upon this description, "And the LORD God formed man of the dust of the ground, and breathed into his nostrils the breath of life; and man became a living being" (Genesis 2:7). Man is a unique creature, formed from the dust of the ground in the natural, but given the breath of life from God's own mouth in the spiritual. This is true of no other creature, not even the angels of heaven.

God created you and me to inhabit both realms of reality, spiritual and physical. This means that, although God's ways and thoughts are higher than our own, He does not intend to keep them from us. The Bible says, "The secret things belong to the Lord our God, but those things which are revealed belong to us and to our children forever, that we may do all the words of this law" (Deuteronomy 29:29).

There are things which God desires to reveal to us, for He does not want us to inhabit the natural realm only. His greater purpose is for us to dwell in spiritual reality, for that is the greater reality. Until we learn to do this, we will not fulfill our destiny and experience our completeness in Christ.

The Bible says, "Eye has not seen, nor ear heard, nor have entered into the heart of man the things which God has prepared for those who love Him. But God has revealed them to us through His Spirit. For the Spirit searches all things, yes, the deep things of God" (1 Corinthians 2:9-10). God is in the business of revealing to us the things He has prepared for us, things of the spiritual realm, even the deep things of God.

> For what man knows the things of a man except the spirit of the man which is in him? Even so no one knows the things of God except the Spirit of God. Now we have received, not the spirit of the world, but the Spirit who is from God, that we might know the things that have been freely given to us by God. These things we also speak, not in words which man's wisdom teaches but which the Holy Spirit teaches, comparing spiritual things with spiritual. But the natural man does not receive the things of the Spirit of God, for they are foolishness to him; nor can he know them, because they are spiritually discerned. (1 Corinthians 2:11-14)

Spirit to Spirit

How does God reveal these things to us? By His Spirit. Because we are spiritual beings, God can communicate with us Spirit to spirit. The Bible says, "The spirit of a man is the lamp of the LORD, searching all the inner depths of his heart" (Proverbs 20:27). A lamp enlightens, or reveals things. The human spirit is a lamp by which God reveals things to us by His own Spirit.

Jesus promised to send the Holy Spirit to all those who receive Him. The Spirit comes so we can know and experience all the things God has freely given us. He teaches us, communicating spiritual-realm truths to us in spiritual-realm ways.

This applies even to the Bible. We can read the words of Scripture and, through principles of interpretation, arrive at a natural-level understanding of what it means. But it takes the Holy Spirit to wake us up to the depth of meaning that is in Scripture, to bring us to a conviction of the truth of God's Word, and to lead us into the actual experience of the things God has prepared for us. Unless the Spirit reveals these things to us, we are living only according to the principles of the natural realm, and not in the greater reality of the spiritual realm. Fortunately, God is more than willing to give us revelation by His Spirit. But are we ready to receive?

Born from Above

Jesus said, "You must be born again," literally, from above (John 3:7). This is a spiritual birth, from the spiritual realm, by the Spirit of God. Although we were created as spiritual beings in the beginning, we were separated from God because of sin. That is spiritual death. The good news of the Gospel is that "God, who is rich in mercy, because of His great love with which He loved us, even when we were dead in trespasses, made us alive together with Christ" (Ephesians 2:4-5).

We receive this new life by faith in Jesus Christ. This is the new birth, a birth from above, from the spiritual realm, from the Spirit of God. It means that now we can receive revelation from the Holy Spirit of all the things God has prepared for us. Now we can begin to experience the deep things of God. Now we can begin to live our lives in, and from, the greater realities of the spiritual realm.

Dear Lord,

Thank You for the richness of Your mercy and the greatness of Your love. When I was dead in trespasses and sins, You loved me and sent Jesus to take my sins upon Himself and carry them to the Cross. Thank You for the new birth from above, and for sending the Holy Spirit. Reveal to my spirit, by Your Spirit, all the wonderful things You have prepared for me. Show me the deep things of God and teach me how to walk in the greater realities of the spiritual realm.

In Jesus' name, Amen.

Having Dominion

Then God blessed them, and God said to them,
"Be fruitful and multiply; fill the earth and subdue it;
have dominion over the fish of the sea,
over the birds of the air, and over
every living thing that
moves on the earth."
(Genesis 1:28)

Have you ever wondered how Adam and Eve were to subdue the earth and have dominion over it? It would not be by toil or the sweat of their brow—that was not part of the mandate, but part of the curse when they fell into sin (Genesis 3:17-19). So what was God's plan for them to accomplish these things?

In order to answer that question, let's first take a look at who they were. In Genesis 1:26, God said, "Let Us make man in Our image, according to Our likeness; let them have dominion over the fish of the sea, over the birds of the air, and over the cattle, over all the earth and over every creeping thing that creeps on the earth." That's just what God did: "So God created man in His own image; in the image of God He created him; male and female He created them" (v. 27).

Who were Adam and Eve? They were beings created upon the earth in the image and likeness of God. Whenever anything in the earth would look upon them, they would behold the image of God. Not only did Adam and Eve bear the image of God on earth, but they were also given dominion over all the earth and everything in it. This was the authority of God, given to them from heaven, to exercise the will of God on the earth.

Let's break out Genesis 1:28. First, we see that God blessed them. You and I often say "God bless you," and don't mean much by it— we are merely being courteous. But when the Bible says, "God blessed them," it is telling us about something very dynamic, for the blessing of God is actually an empowerment. It is the favor of God and all of heaven coming together on behalf of the one being blessed. In blessing the man and woman, God was saying, "I am releasing all My power and provision to assist you and bring you into the destiny for which I have created you."

Second, the Bible says, "And God said to them ..." Notice that it did not simply say, "Then God blessed them and said to them ..." There were two distinct acts: God blessed, then God said. This is important when we consider the context of Genesis: God created the heavens and the earth by what He said. Whenever God speaks, He is creating and establishing something. That is the very nature of His Word. When "God said to them ...," He was establishing something in them.

What was it that God was establishing when He said, "Be fruitful and multiply?" The word "fruitful" has to do with increase by reproduction. Multiplication also refers to increase, of course, but the Hebrew word for "multiply" can also carry the idea of being in authority. We usually understand "Be fruitful and multiply" to mean, simply, that Adam and Eve were to have many children, but there is much more to this mandate than that.

What was to increase and multiply in abundance on the earth?

The first couple could only increase and multiply that which they were and possessed. Since they bore the image of God, God charged them to increase, multiply and fill the earth with His image. They also were being given dominion—authority over the earth—and that was to multiply and abound, as well. This would happen as they fathered and nurtured their children in the purposes of God. Their children would bear the image of God and extend the authority of God throughout the earth. In turn, these would father and nurture their own children in the same way.

Next, God told them, "Fill the earth and subdue it." To fill means to accomplish and confirm something, to bring it to fullness and completion. To subdue means to bring into subjection. Man was created to multiply the image and authority of God on the earth, to bring the earth and everything in it to completion, fully in line with the will and purpose of God.

"Have dominion," God said. They were to rule over the fish, the birds, and every creature. Indeed, God gave them dominion over the whole earth. That's a tall order. Just how were they to accomplish it? To answer that, we need to consider how God Himself did things, since Adam and Eve were created in His image.

How did God create and establish things? By His Word. "And God said ..." God operates by His Word, but is that how He created Adam and Eve to operate? Look in Genesis 2:7, which is a close-up account of how God created Adam: "And the LORD God formed man of the dust of the ground, and breathed into his nostrils the breath of life; and man became a living being."

Man is a creature who is unique in all the universe. He alone has the breath of God in him. Literally, God puffed the breath of life into Adam's nostrils, then Adam became a *nephesh chayyim*, a "living being." *Chayyim* is the word for living, but Adam was not alive with the life with which the animals of Genesis 1 were said to be living. There was a qualitative difference to the life that was in

45

him: He was living solely and especially because the breath of life from God's own mouth was in him.

In other Bible passages, the word for "being," *nephesh,* is often translated as "mind" (for example, Genesis 23:8 and Deuteronomy 18:6). In the context of what God did and what man became, *nephesh* refers to more than mere existence; it involves the capacity for conscious thought and self-awareness.

There are a couple of other words translated as "mind" in the Old Testament which help us understand this connection even more. The Hebrew word for "spirit," *ruach,* is often used to refer to "wind," and even "breath." But it, also, is used as a word for "mind" (Genesis 26:35). The breath that God breathed into Adam's nostrils was actually the Holy Spirit, giving life to Adam's body. But we can also say that what God breathed into Adam was the mind of God.

Another interesting word in this regard is the Hebrew word *peh.* In Leviticus 24:12, it is translated as "mind." But it literally refers to the mouth as a means of blowing. God, with His mouth, blew the breath of life into Adam's nostrils (this certainly gives a new meaning to the term "mind-blowing").

God says, "My thoughts are not your thoughts, nor are your ways My ways" (Isaiah 55:8). But that does not mean that we cannot know God's thoughts. Indeed, we were created with the capacity to know the mind of God, to understand His ways and walk in them. Though Adam fell, we still have this capacity to think the thoughts of God after Him, if we have experienced the new birth by the Holy Spirit. For as Paul says:

> "Eye has not seen, nor ear heard, nor have entered into the heart of man the things which God has prepared for those who love Him." But God has revealed them to us through His Spirit. For the Spirit searches all things, yes, the deep things of God. For what man knows the things of a man except the spirit of the man which is in him? Even so no one knows the things of God except the Spirit of

God. (1 Corinthians 2:9-11)

The *Targum Onkelos*, an ancient Aramaic translation and commentary on the Hebrew scriptures, also has something very interesting to say about Genesis 2:7. The commentator concludes that God blew into the man's nostrils and the man became a *speaking spirit*. Not only did Adam bear the image of God, and the authority of God, but he was also created as a speaking spirit, to breathe forth words, even as God does. Now, follow on in Genesis 2 and see how this began to play out with Adam's first assignment:

> Out of the ground the LORD God formed every beast of the field and every bird of the air, and brought them to Adam to see what he would call them. And whatever Adam called each living creature, that was its name. (Genesis 2:19)

Remember that God gave Adam authority over the beasts and the birds, and now He brought them to Adam, for Adam to begin exercising that authority. How did Adam do it? By giving each creature a name. He called them, and whatever he called them, that was their name.

Today, we are prone to miss the significance of this because we often think of our names as being incidental, having no particular meaning or value within themselves. But in the plan of God, names are very important. They are words by which destinies are established. For example, in the midst of the darkness in Genesis 1:2, God called forth Light. He named it, and by naming, established its function. Or take Abraham as another example. Abraham was old and childless, and his wife was far beyond child-bearing years. Yet God promised that he would be the father of numberless descendants. So God gave him the name Abraham, which means "father of a multitude." Every time Abraham or Sarah spoke the word of this name, they were calling forth Abraham's God-given destiny.

Names are important. They are words brought forth by breathing, speaking spirits. When Adam gave names to the animals, he was not merely discovering and exposing their identities and characteristics; he was actually forging, by his words, the purpose, meaning and destiny of each one of those creatures. He was exercising his God-given authority, speaking forth words with the breath of life that came from God's own lips. Or, to put it another way, he was "having dominion" over the animals, ruling over them to bring them into line with the plan and purpose of God.

God has not given up on the plan He established in Genesis 1. Today, every believer in Jesus Christ has the authority to fulfill God's mandate:

▸ Multiplying the image of God on the earth by establishing godly families and nurturing relationships.

▸ Filling the earth and bringing it to completion through prayer and faith, calling for the will of God to be done on earth as it is in heaven.

▸ Subduing the earth, bringing it into line with the faith-filled proclamation of the Word of God.

▸ Exercising the dominion of the kingdom of God everywhere we go, through the authority of the name of Jesus (John 16:23-24), the Lord's Prayer (Matthew 6:9-13), binding and loosing (Matthew 18:18), the prayer of agreement (Matthew 18:19), and the Great Commission (Matthew 28:18-20).

God's Word in Your Mouth

With my lips I have declared
all the judgments of Your mouth.
(Psalm 119:13)

*O*ur lips are sacred vessels—they were made to declare the Word of the Lord! The psalm writer said, "With my lips I have declared all the judgments of Your mouth." Now, he wasn't talking about raining down condemnation on everyone and everything. In Psalm 119, the word "judgment" is used as a synonym for the "commandments," "statutes," "testimonies," "precepts," "ordinances," the "laws" and "words" of God. Rather, he was talking about declaring, proclaiming and celebrating the Word of God, because that is the very thing our mouths were created to do.

> Then God said, "Let Us make man in Our image, according to Our likeness; let them have dominion over the fish of the sea, over the birds of the air, and over the cattle, over all the earth and over every creeping thing that creeps on the earth." So God created man in His *own* image; in the image of God He created him; male and female He created them. Then God blessed them, and God said to them, "Be fruitful and multiply; fill the earth and subdue it; have dominion over the fish of the sea, over the birds of the air, and over every living thing that moves on the earth." (Genesis 1:26-28)

Man was created, not only *in* the image of God, but *as* the image of God, so that he might fulfill the divine mandate on the earth. The first assignment God gave Adam was to name the animals (Genesis 2.:19-20). He was to open up his mouth and speak words to them, imparting to them their God-given identities and destinies. Thus Adam was God's administrator, His mouthpiece, speaking on His behalf.

God has always intended for His Word to remain in our mouths. He commanded Joshua,

> This Book of the Law shall not depart from your mouth, but you shall meditate in it day and night, that you may observe to do according to all that is written in it. For then you will make your way prosperous, and then you will have good success. (Joshua 1:8)

We are to meditate on God's Word all the time, literally "muttering" it to ourselves (that's the meaning of the Hebrew word for "meditate"). Whenever we speak, no matter what situation we find ourselves in, we are to speak God's Word and line up our words in agreement with it. We are to do the Word, think the Word, speak the Word. Then we will be prosperous and successful in everything God has called us to do.

The Word of God is always effective. The Bible says, "So shall My word be that goes forth from My mouth; it shall not return to Me void, but it shall accomplish what I please, and it shall prosper in the thing for which I sent it" (Isaiah 55:11). That is why God wants us to keep the Word in our mouths—it comes from Him and is, therefore, full of power to accomplish all His plans and purposes. It is powerful in our mouth, as well, because it comes first from His.

The Ministry of Jesus

Now, let's take a look at the ministry of Jesus to see how He used words. Consider, for example, the story of how He healed Peter's mother-in-law.

Now He arose from the synagogue and entered Simon's house. But Simon's wife's mother was sick with a high fever, and they made request of Him concerning her. So He stood over her and rebuked the fever, and it left her. (Luke 4:38-39)

Notice that Jesus *rebuked* the fever, that is, He spoke words to it—and it left her.

Here's another example: One day, when a powerful windstorm swept over the little boat that carried Jesus and His disciples, the disciples went to the stern of the boat, where Jesus was asleep on a pillow. "Teacher," they said, "do You not care that we are perishing?"

Then He arose and rebuked the wind, and said to the sea, "Peace, be still!" And the wind ceased and there was a great calm. But He said to them, "Why are you so fearful? How is it that you have no faith?" (Mark 4:36-40)

Jesus spoke words of rebuke to the wind. He spoke words of peace and calm over the sea. They obeyed and everything became calm and still because of the words that came from His mouth.

The ministry of Jesus was very effective and successful because of His words. But here is something we need to understand about those words: They were not His own. Rather, He spoke only those things He heard the Father saying.

I do nothing on my own but speak just what the Father has taught me. (John 8:28 *NIV*)

For I did not speak of my own accord, but the Father who sent me commanded me what to say and how to say it … So whatever I say is just what the Father has told me to say." (John 12:49-50 *NIV*)

Everything Jesus said and did came straight from the Father. He did not act or speak outside of the parameters of what He heard the Father do and say. If the Father said it, Jesus said it. If the Father was not saying it, then neither was Jesus. This was the "secret" of

His effectiveness—complete and total dependence on the Father. If the Lord Jesus Himself was careful to speak only those things that come from the Father, how much more careful ought we be to speak only those things.

Idle Words or God's Words?

This is a very important issue, for Jesus warned the scribes and Pharisees, "But I say to you that for every idle word men may speak, they will give account of it in the day of judgment. For by your words you will be justified, and by your words you will be condemned" (Matthew 12:36-37). Idle words are words that do not line up with what the Word of God says. They have no power for good, and do nothing to accomplish the purposes of God.

The truth about words is that they accomplish things. They may accomplish good things, they may accomplish bad things, but they do accomplish *something*. Even the words you think you did not mean may actually accomplish things, because Jesus said that the mouth speaks out of the abundance, or overflow, of the heart (Luke 6:46).

Some people go around damning people and things in the name of God. They either mean it or they don't. If they mean it, then they are speaking blasphemy, because God is not in the damning business, and they are attributing to Him that which does not belong to Him. If they don't mean it, then their words are idle, and they will have to give account of them before God anyway.

God's Word in Your Mouth and in Your Heart

There is another way words may be idle, and that is when they are not mixed with faith. You see, there is a connection between your faith and your words, just as there is a connection between your heart and your mouth.

But what does it say? "The word is near you, in your mouth and in your heart" (that is, the word of faith which we preach): that if you confess with your mouth the Lord Jesus and believe in your heart that God has raised Him from the dead, you will be saved. For with the heart one believes unto righteousness, and with the mouth confession is made unto salvation. (Romans 10:8-10)

The essence of confession is agreement. To confess the Lord Jesus means to agree that He is indeed Lord. When you confess the Word of God, you are coming into line with it, setting yourself in agreement with it.

The Bible says that with the heart you believe and with the mouth you confess. That is how faith works: You take God's Word and you speak it out. It is not just the Word by itself, though, but the Word mixed with faith, that is effective and powerful.

Speaking to Mountains

When the Word is mixed with faith, it is just as powerful in your mouth as it is in God's mouth. Jesus taught that to the disciples toward the end of His ministry.

> Now the next day, when they had come out from Bethany, He was hungry. And seeing from afar a fig tree having leaves, He went to see if perhaps He would find something on it. When He came to it, He found nothing but leaves, for it was not the season for figs. In response Jesus said to it, "Let no one eat fruit from you ever again." And His disciples heard it. (Mark 11:12-14)

> Now in the morning, as they passed by, they saw the fig tree dried up from the roots. And Peter, remembering, said to Him, "Rabbi, look! The fig tree which You cursed has withered away." So Jesus answered and said to them, "Have faith in God. For assuredly, I say to you, whoever says to this mountain, 'Be removed and be cast into the sea,' and does not doubt in his heart, but believes that those things he says will be done, he will have whatever he says.

Therefore I say to you, whatever things you ask when you pray, believe that you receive them, and you will have them. (Mark 11:20-24)

Notice that Jesus begins His answer with "Have faith in God." Literally, in the Greek text, this is "Have faith *of* God." That is, have the faith that comes from God. When God speaks, He has an expectation that it is going to be done. Jesus spoke to the fig tree and expected that word to be fulfilled. He said only those things He heard the Father saying, and He mixed it with faith. He had faith in God, and He exercised that faith by what He said.

Speaking to mountains and expecting to see results is a God thing. It is taking the words that come from Him and mixing them with the faith that comes from Him. When you do that, you will always get the results that come from Him.

Become a World-Changer

Here is what happens when you determine that your lips were made to declare the Word of God: You get God-results. Now, I'm not suggesting that you have to go around speaking only Scripture all day long, but I am saying that every single word that comes out of your mouth needs to be in alignment with what God says, and not contrary to it.

If there is only one thing you learn this year, let it be this: Speak only those things that are in agreement with the Word of God. When you do, it will not only change your life, but it will turn you into a world-changer.

The Shadow of Glory

They brought the sick out into the streets and laid them on beds
and couches, that at least the shadow of Peter passing
by might fall on some of them.
(Acts 5:15)

The Bible has much to say about shadows. Some of the shadows it talks about are negative. The phrase "shadow of death," is used quite often, most famously in the Shepherd Psalm: "Yea, though I walk through the valley of the shadow of death, I will fear no evil" (Psalm 23:4).

"Shadow" is also used as a metaphor for the brevity and transience of life. In Job 8:9, for example, we find this assessment: "For we were born yesterday, and know nothing, because our days on earth are a shadow." Here, shadows are seen as fleeting and insubstantial.

In the New Testament, James uses the figure of a shadow to contrast with the eternal stability and faithfulness of God: "Every good gift and every perfect gift is from above, and comes down from the Father of lights, with whom there is no variation or shadow of turning" (James 1:17). God is not fleeting in any of His ways. His shadow does not shift or change.

The Scriptures also reveal to us shadows that are absolutely wonderful—in fact, they show us shadows which are divine. For example, we find "shadow" used to speak of refuge—the divine protection we have in God. The psalmwriter says, "Keep me as the apple of Your eye; hide me under the shadow of your wings" (Psalm 17:8). "How precious is Your lovingkindness, O God! Therefore the children of men put their trust under the shadow of Your wings" (Psalm 36:7). "In the shadow of Your wings I will make my refuge" (Psalm 57:1). "He who dwells in the secret place of the Most High shall abide under the shadow of the Almighty" (Psalm 91:1).

The divine shadow is not only a place of refuge, but also of refreshing and delight. "Like an apple tree among the tree of the woods, so is my beloved among the sons. I sat down in His shade with great delight, and His fruit was sweet to my taste" (Song of Solomon 2:3).

Sometimes "shadow" is used figuratively of prophetic things, pointing toward the person and work of the Lord Jesus Christ. For example, Paul counseled, "Let no one judge you in food or in drink, or regarding a festival or a new moon or sabbaths, which are a shadow of things to come, but the substance is of Christ" (Colossians 2:16-17). The author of Hebrews, demonstrating the superiority of Christ, speaks of the Aaronic priesthood as those "who serve the copy and shadow of the heavenly things" of which Christ is the fulfillment (Hebrews 8:5). Even the Law of Moses was described as "having a shadow of the good things to come," things which are now realized in Christ (Hebrews 10:1).

In one of Jesus' parables, a shadow reveals the blessing of God's presence, His power and glory graciously reaching out to the world:

> Then He said, "To what shall we liken the kingdom of God? Or with what parable shall we picture it? It is like a mustard seed which, when it is sown on the ground, is smaller than all the seeds on earth; but when it is sown, it grows up and becomes greater than all herbs, and shoots out large branches, so that the birds of the air may nest under its shade." (Mark 4:30-32. The KJV says,

"So that the fowls of the air may lodge under the *shadow* of it.")

The Kingdom of God casts a powerful and pervasive shadow, so it should come as no surprise that the sons and daughters of that kingdom are also found to cast shadows of divine refuge and restoration. That is exactly what we find throughout the Book of Acts, especially in chapter 5, which explicitly employs the language of shadow:

> And through the hands of the apostles many signs and wonders were done among the people. And they were all with one accord in Solomon's Porch. Yet none of the rest dared join them, but the people esteemed them highly. And believers were increasingly added to the Lord, multitudes of both men and women, so that they brought the sick out into the streets and laid them on beds and couches, that at least the shadow of Peter passing by might fall on some of them. Also a multitude gathered from the surrounding cities to Jerusalem, bringing sick people and those who were tormented by unclean spirits, and they were all healed. (Acts 5:12-16)

Glory Overshadowing

The Greek word for "shadow" in the New Testament is *skia*, and means what we normally associate with "shadow." But there are a couple of other Greek words built on this root which intensify the concept into divine proportions.

The first one is *kataskiazo*, which literally means "to shadow down." We find it only one time in the New Testament, at Hebrews 9:5, to describe the Ark of the Covenant: "And above it were the cherubim of glory overshadowing the mercy seat." The cherubim are angelic beings who represent the glory of God and safeguard His holiness. We discover this in Genesis, when Adam and Eve fell into sin and were expelled from the Garden of Eden. Cherubim were posted, and a flaming sword, to guard the way to the tree of life (Genesis 3:24). This was actually a mercy shown to the first couple, that they might not be confirmed in everlasting rebellion.

In the Ark of the Covenant, the cherubim are depicted as the glory of God "shadowing down" to the place of mercy. This glory comes down from heaven, from the throne room of God to reveal the mercy of God in salvation, healing, deliverance and restoration on earth. This glory is the shadow that is cast by the Kingdom of God.

There is another word, *episkiazo*, which builds on the root word *skia*, and is generally rendered as "overshadow." We find it only five times in the New Testament, but in each case it describes a powerful, even tangible, manifestation of the glory of God on earth. It first occurs in the Annunciation passage, where the angel of the Lord visits the Virgin Mary:

> And the angel answered and said to her, "The Holy Spirit will come upon you, and the power of the Highest will overshadow you; therefore, also, that Holy One who is to be born will be called the Son of God." (Luke 1:35)

It was in this powerful overshadowing that the Holy Spirit came upon Mary, and the Lord Jesus was conceived in her womb. Heaven and earth came together in that moment, and the glory of the Father was acutely revealed. The result was the Kingdom of God breaking into the world through the birth of the infant King.

The next three uses of *episkiazo* are found in the three Gospel accounts of the Transfiguration (Matthew 17, Mark 9 and Luke 9). These are parallel passages, so it will be sufficient for our purposes to look at only one, Matthew 17:

> Now after six days Jesus took Peter, James, and John his brother, led them up on a high mountain by themselves; and He was transfigured before them. His face shone like the sun, and His clothes became as white as the light. And behold, Moses and Elijah appeared to them, talking with Him. Then Peter answered and

said to Jesus, "Lord, it is good for us to be here; if You wish, let us make here three tabernacles: one for You, one for Moses, and one for Elijah." While he was still speaking, behold, a bright cloud overshadowed them; and suddenly a voice came out of the cloud, saying, "This is My beloved Son, in whom I am well pleased. Hear Him!" (Matthew 17:1-5)

Some translations say that the bright cloud *enveloped* them. In other words, it did not simply hover over them but was all around them. It invaded their atmosphere. Not only that, it was tangible to them. They experienced it as a brilliant cloud of light, a cloud of God's glory made visible to them. The power and goodness of God—the very substance of heaven itself—was entering their world, materializing before their eyes. Now they could see why Jesus was transfigured before them, why His face and clothes shone so intensely.

We discover the final use of *episkiazo* in Acts chapter 5: "They brought the sick out into the streets and laid them on beds and couches, that at least the shadow of Peter passing by might fall on some of them" (Acts 5:15). The word "shadow" in this verse is the Greek *skia*. But there is another shadow present, found behind the words "fall on" (the KJV shows it as "overshadow"). This is *episkiazo*—the shadow of glory!

The believers at Jerusalem came and brought their sick before Peter. They had heard the gospel message he preached, "how God anointed Jesus of Nazareth with the Holy Spirit and with power, who went about doing good and healing all who were oppressed by the devil, for God was with Him" (Acts 10:38). They were aware of what had happened at Pentecost, how the same Spirit who anointed Jesus also anointed His disciples with power to bear evidence of who Jesus is and what He came to do (Acts 1:8). They had also just seen what happened to Ananias and Sapphira and recognized that Peter and the apostles came with the authority of heaven (Acts 5:1-11). Then they witnessed for themselves the many signs and wonders that were being performed by the apostles, with Peter prominently featured among them.

It was not merely Peter's natural shadow they were interested in, for there was no power in that to accomplish anything, but it served as an indicator that a far greater shadow was passing by. The Kingdom of God was breaking into their world, and they desired to be overshadowed by it. They wanted to be surrounded by the glory of God, where the will of God is done on earth as it is in heaven. They hoped to be enveloped by the power of God, to be changed by it, saved by it, healed by it. So they came and brought their sick ones and laid them where Peter was passing by, in order that his divine shadow, the shadow of God's anointing which was on Peter, might overshadow them, and the glory of God might fall on them with healing power.

We often think of a shadow as a place of darkness, but perhaps it will be more fruitful for us to remember that a shadow is a place that is surrounded by light. Identifying shadows with light rather than darkness, we can begin to understand how to cast the shadows of the kingdom of God: We cast a shadow whenever we are surrounded by the light.

In the case of Peter's shadow, darkness was not only surrounded by the light but was overcome by it as well. Sickness, disease, and even demonic oppression were wiped out by this shadow: "Also a multitude gathered from the surrounding cities to Jerusalem, bringing sick people and those who were tormented by unclean spirits, and they were all healed" (Acts 5:16).

Understanding Darkness

Before we go any further, there is something fundamental we need to understand: Darkness is not the presence of something, but the absence of something. Darkness is not a thing in itself, it has no real existence on its own. Darkness is nothing more than the absence of light. That is why you can turn on a light switch, but you can't turn on a dark switch. You can shine a light in the darkness, but you can't shine a dark in the lightness. Light is something; darkness is nothing but the absence of light.

This is why it is impossible for darkness to overcome light. Wherever light is present, darkness is no more. Have you ever noticed that when you go home to a dark house and turn on the light, the darkness immediately disappears? Have you ever wondered about where that darkness goes? Does it push outside the doors and windows and pile up with all the other darkness that is already out there, making it even more dark outside? Of course not! When you turn on the light, the darkness is simply gone. It has disappeared and is no more. That is because light thoroughly overcomes darkness.

Now that we have more understanding about darkness in the physical realm, let's consider it in the spiritual realm. We might talk about spiritual darkness as sin, evil, poverty, sickness, death, and so on. Just as physical darkness in not a thing in itself, the same can be said about spiritual darkness. It is not the presence of something, but the absence of something.

For example, sin is the absence of righteousness. In both the Old and New Testaments, the word for "sin" literally means to "miss the mark" at which one is aiming. In the context of Scripture, sin is missing the mark of the righteousness of God. That is, it is the absence of righteousness. We can follow through in this same way with all the elements of spiritual darkness. Evil is simply the lack of good. Poverty is the absence of provision. Sickness is a deficiency of health, and death is the total lack of life.

Understanding Light

Now let's talk about light. The first thing we need to understand is that God *is* light. The Bible says, "This is the message which we have heard from Him and declare to you, that God is light and in Him there is no darkness at all" (1 John 1:5). God is light and in Him is no lack or deficiency of any kind.

Not only is God Himself light, He is also the source of all light, both in the natural and in the spiritual. James calls Him "the Father of lights, with whom there is no variation or shadow of turning" (James 1:17). Genesis teaches that, on the very first day of Creation, God said, "Let there be light," and there was light (Genesis 1:3). God is Himself the light of creation, shining even before the sun, moon and stars were created. He is also the light of the Consummation, the completion of all things. John the Revelator describes the New Jerusalem coming down to earth and says, "There shall be no night there: They need no lamp nor light of the sun, for the Lord God gives them light" (Revelation 22:5).

Light is redemptive. Every time we find "light" mentioned in Scripture, it is bringing forth something good, introducing or restoring what has been lacking. That is why Jesus, whose very name depicts salvation in all its aspects, is described as light. "In Him was life, and the life was the light of men. And the light shines in the darkness, and the darkness did not comprehend [overcome] it" (John 1:4-5). John the Baptist gave witness to Jesus, that He was "the true Light which gives light to every man coming into the world" (John 1:8).

God is light, Jesus is light, and all those who receive the Lord Jesus are called children of light. "For you were once darkness, but now you are light in the Lord. Walk as children of light" (Ephesians 5:8). "You are all sons of light and sons of the day. We are not of the night nor of darkness" (1 Thessalonians 5:5). "He has delivered us from the power of darkness and conveyed us into the kingdom of the Son of His love" (Colossians 1:13).

Once we were of the darkness, but now we are light in the Lord. The function of light is to shine and dispel the darkness. That is exactly what happened with Peter. He learned how to have a shadow which shined with the glory of God, and dispelled the darkness around him. The power of God was powerfully made known through him. The result is that people were saved, people were healed, people were set free.

It is like what happened when the woman with the issue of blood came and touched the hem of Jesus' garment. She was healed. She felt the healing power of God come into her body, making her whole. At the same time, Jesus felt the healing power of God flow forth from His body (Luke 8:43-48). Many others received healing in the exact same way. The Gospel of Mark, in language that is reminiscent of Acts 5:15, says, "Wherever He entered, into villages, cities, or the country, they laid the sick in the marketplaces, and begged Him that they might just touch the hem of His garment. And as many as touched Him were made well" (Mark 6:56). Was this not the "overshadowing" of the glory of God?

Think again of Paul in Acts 19: "Now God worked unusual miracles by the hands of Paul, so that even handkerchiefs or aprons were brought from his body to the sick, and the diseases left them and the evil spirits went out of them" (Acts 19:11-12). The power of God came forth in real and substantial ways, restoring health and freedom where it had been lacking. Was this not also an "overshadowing" of God's glory and goodness dispelling the darkness?

How to Have a Shadow

Since all those who receive the Lord Jesus Christ are called children of light, it must be possible for us to live in the light, to shine the light in dark places and to reflect the light of God's glory, even focusing it like a laser in powerful ways. In other words, it is possible for us to overshadow others with the life-changing power of God, to bring salvation, healing, freedom and the peace of God into their lives. Here are four principles by which we can begin:

1. Walk in the light.

This is the message which we have heard from Him and declare to you, that God is light and in Him is no darkness at all. If we say that we have fellowship with Him, and walk in darkness, we lie and do not practice the truth. But if we walk in the light as He is in the light, we have fellowship with one another, and the blood of Jesus Christ His son cleanses us from all sin. (1 John 1:7)

God is light. When we walk in the light as He is in the light, we experience close fellowship with Him, and the cleansing power of Jesus' blood. The overshadowing glory is the glory of God Himself. It is all about Him. As we walk with Him we will be enveloped in His glory, and we will cast the shadow of His glory everywhere we go.

2. Walk in love.

Again, a new commandment I write to you, which thing is true in Him and in you, because the darkness is passing away, and the true light is already shining. He who says he is in the light, and hates his brother, is in darkness until now. He who loves his brother abides in the light, and there is no cause for stumbling in him. But he who hates his brother is in darkness and walks in darkness, and does not know where he is going, because the darkness has blinded his eyes. (1 John 2:8-10)

The Bible says, "He who does not love does not know God, for God is love" (1 John 4:8). God is love, and the nature of love is to give and serve. "For God so loved the world that He gave His only begotten Son" (John 3:16). "The Son of Man did not come to be served, but to serve, and to give His life a ransom for many" (Mark 10:45).

When we learn to walk in love toward others—to give and serve and lay down our lives for them—we will experience God and His love in deeper, more intimate ways, and we will be walking in the light of His glory, casting the shadow of His healing love wherever it is needed.

3. Walk in the Word.

The Psalm writer said, "Your Word is a lamp to my feet and a light to my path" (Psalm 119:105). "The entrance of your words gives light; it gives understanding to the simple" (Psalm 119:130). In fact, Psalms 1, 19 and 119 all speak in depth about the Word of God and how walking in obedience to it brings the power and blessing of heaven into our lives.

God's Word is a light that shines in the darkness, as Peter well understood: "And so we have the prophetic Word confirmed, which you do well to heed as a light that shines in a dark place, until the day dawns and the morning star rises in your hearts" (2 Peter 1:19). When we receive the Word of God in faith, and the morning star (Jesus) rises in our hearts, the shadow of His glory begins to release into our lives.

4. Walk in Worship.

The Bible says, "A fire shall always be burning on the altar; it shall never go out" (Leviticus 6:13). The fire on the altar is the light of worship. It never goes out, but burns day and night, casting its light on all that surrounds.

In the tabernacle of David there were no walls (1 Chronicles 16), so all could behold the Ark of the Covenant and the glory of God's presence. The fire on the alter, and the praises of God's people burned continually before the Lord, and the shadow of His glory covered the land and its inhabitants with His blessing.

Worship is speaking forth and declaring the "worth-ship," or worthiness of God. We glorify God by showing and proclaiming His goodness. David said, "Oh, taste and see that the LORD is good" (Psalm 34:8).

Ruth Ward Heflin understood this connection between worship and the manifestation of God's glory, and offered this counsel: "Praise until the Spirit of Worship comes. Worship until the Glory comes. Then stand in the Glory."

As we stand in the glory of God, the fire on the altar of our hearts burning brightly with His love, we cannot help but cast shadows that bring the healing, freedom and peace of God into the lives of others.

Bearers of the glory

The shadow of glory has not passed away, for the Kingdom of God has not passed away—and it never shall! In all the centuries in the history of the Church, countless multitudes have been overshadowed by the divine glory, enveloped by the power of God that saves, heals and sets the captives free. It shows up wherever those who believe in the Lord Jesus Christ begin to understand who they are in Him and walk in the authority He has given them.

The fact is, we are all bearers of the glory, if we know the Lord Jesus Christ, for the glory which the Father gave to Jesus is the exact same glory Jesus has given to us (John 17:22). That is why the Bible says, "As He is, so are we in this world" (1 John 4:17). Therefore, we should expect to walk with the same shadow of glory that accompanied Peter, for it is the glory of the Lord Jesus Himself.

Heaven on Earth

𝓞n the book of Ephesians, the apostle Paul speaks five times of "heavenly places." That is how the King James Version and many other translations render it—often with the word "places" in italics to indicate that it was added, for clarity, by the translators. A few translations have it as "heavenly realms," and the Amplified Bible alternates between "realm" and "sphere." However, the most literal reading of the Greek text is simply "in the heavenlies."

- "Blessed be the God and Father of our Lord Jesus Christ, who has blessed us with every spiritual blessing *in the heavenlies* in Christ" (Ephesians 1:3).

- Paul prayed that we might know the greatness of God's power toward us, the same working of power "which He worked in Christ when He raised Him from the dead and seated Him at His right hand *in the heavenlies*" (Ephesians 1:20).

- God has "raised us up together, and made us sit together *in the heavenlies* in Christ Jesus" (Ephesians 2:6).

- Paul speaks of God's intention "that now the manifold wisdom of God might be made known by the church

to the principalities and powers *in the heavenlies*"
(Ephesians 3:10).

▸ "For we do not wrestle against flesh and blood, but
against principalities, against powers, against the rulers
of the darkness of this age, against spiritual hosts of wick-
edness *in the heavenlies*" (Ephesians 6:12).

The Heavenlies

We tend to think of heaven as a place far, far away, so we have
difficulty understanding what Paul is talking about when he speaks
about us in relation to the heavenlies. For example, Paul declares
that we possess every spiritual blessing in the heavenlies. But when
we think of heaven at a distance, those blessings don't seem to be
very real or relevant to us. They merely become something to be
experienced in the next life, not in this one.

The Bible says that Jesus is seated at the right hand of God, in
the heavenlies. But when we think of this in terms of place, it makes
Jesus seem very distant, and we wonder how He can be present in
our midst at the same time He is so far away up in heaven.

If that is not enough, Paul throws us a real curve ball when he
says that God has raised us up and made us sit in the heavenlies
with Jesus. This is not something God *will* do, but something He
has done already. But how can that be? How can we be in two
places at the same time—both here on earth and seated with Christ
at the right hand of God in the heavenlies? It is confusing to us
when we think merely in terms of place.

But what if we began to think of "the heavenlies" in terms of
realm or dimension instead? That would require some reorienta-
tion in our thinking, but the effort would be well rewarded. Our
confusion would dissipate, and the distance between heaven and
earth would begin to disappear.

It is not very hard to do, especially with the help of the Holy Spirit. In fact, we already have a little bit of experience thinking in terms of dimension. We generally understand the world in three dimensions—height, width and length. Nobody ever wonders how we can have height and width and length all at the same time. We even think of time as a dimension of physical existence, and easily understand that we move through the three dimensions of space as well as the dimension of time.

We need to learn to think of heaven in the same sort of way— not so much as a higher *place*, but as a higher *dimension* of existence, a greater *realm* of reality. When we do, the dynamics of Scripture become much more clear, and real, to us. We also begin to experience the salvation of God as a present reality, and not simply as a promise for the future.

Heaven on Earth

Jesus made a very important statement to Nicodemus: "Most assuredly, I say to you, unless one is born again, he cannot see the kingdom of God" (John 3:3). The Greek for "born again" literally means "born *from above.*" That is, born from that higher realm, where the kingdom of God comes from. In other words, the only way anyone can become part of the kingdom of God is to be born there at its source. Heaven has no department of "Immigration and Naturalization Services." We belong there solely by birth, which happens when we receive the Lord Jesus Christ by faith—we become native-born citizens of that higher realm. As Paul said, "Our citizenship is in heaven" (Philippians 3:20).

This changes everything! It is why Jesus' sermon on the mount is so *radical* (from Latin *radix*, "of the root"). He was talking about belonging to a different realm. He was preaching from a perspective rooted in a higher dimension of reality—the heavenlies. Those who come in "poverty of spirit," that is, depending upon God alone, belong to the kingdom of heaven. Those who walk in the humility and gentleness of heaven, not in the pride and violence of the world, are the ones who inherit the earth. Those who are undivided in their affections, firmly embracing the purposes of God, are the ones who see His face.

Jesus said, "Lay up for yourselves treasure in heaven … for where your treasure is, there your heart will be also" (Matthew 6:20-21). Paul said something similar: "Seek those things which are above, where Christ is sitting at the right hand of God. Set your mind on things above, not on things on the earth" (Colossians 3:1-2).

Jesus is seated in the heavenlies (Ephesians 1:20) and we are seated there with Him (Ephesians 2:6). So it makes perfect sense to lay up our treasure there, to seek those things which are above—to set our hearts and minds on the heavenlies. For that is where we are seated, and our hearts and minds should certainly be wherever *we* are.

We still live *in* the natural, earthly realm, but we live *from* the heavenly, spiritual realm, where we are seated with Jesus. That is also where we are blessed with every spiritual blessing. We bring forth these blessings and live them out in the natural realm as well as the spiritual. That is why we lay up treasure for ourselves in heaven, so it can truly become of use to us upon the earth. It is made holy to the Lord and bears the substance of His provision from that higher realm all the way down to where it is needed in the natural.

This also enlarges our understanding of the "Lord's Prayer" (Matthew 6:9-13). When we pray, "Your kingdom come," we are not asking for it to come *to* us, we are praying for it to come *through* us. "Your kingdom come" is in the imperative voice. That is, it is a command. We are not petitioning heaven to send it, we are bringing it forth by our intercession in the name of Jesus. It is not a plaintiff cry but a confident exercise of the authority of Jesus.

"Your will be done on earth as it is in heaven." In the same way, we bring the things of heaven forth to manifest upon the earth. This also is in the imperative voice.

The grammatical tense of "Your kingdom come" means to "come and continue coming." Likewise, "Your will be done" means to "be done and continue being done." We inhabit both realms, heaven and earth, and we are to be in a constant flow of communication between them, praying continually and constantly manifesting the kingdom of God and the things of heaven upon the earth. It is like Jacob's ladder, with angels always ascending and descending.

We find this same authority later on in Matthew, where Jesus once again speaks about believers manifesting the things of heaven upon the earth:

> Assuredly, I say to you, whatever you bind on earth will be bound in heaven, and whatever you loose on earth will be loosed in heaven. Again I say to you that if two of you agree on earth concerning anything that they ask, it will be done for them by My Father in heaven. For where two or three are gathered together in My name, I am there in the midst of them. (Matthew 18:18-20)

There is a powerful connection between heaven and earth—and we are it! Whatever we bind or restrain on earth is also bound in heaven. Whatever we loose or set free on earth is also loosed in heaven. That is because, as believers in the Lord Jesus Christ, we now belong to heaven. When we agree with each other concerning a matter, we are agreeing with heaven. We stand upon the earth, but we are seated in the heavenlies, in Jesus. God honors the name of Jesus, and when we come into agreement with His name and His purposes, our Father in heaven honors our request upon the earth.

In this way, we experience heaven on earth. In the higher, heavenly realm, we sit with Jesus as He rules and reigns. In the natural, earthly realm, we are a colony of heaven—the kingdom of God

Living in the Blessing

*W*ould you like to be happy? Live a long and fruitful life? Enjoy success and prosperity in every area of your life? Would you like to have the power of heaven on your side? That is what the blessing is about.

The Bible has much to say about blessing. Blessing is from the Lord. It comes down from heaven and manifests on the earth. It is the divine enablement that brings success, prosperity, fruitfulness and long life.

God has blessing for His people. Not just *a* blessing, but *the* blessing. You see, *a* blessing opens up the window of heaven into a particular aspect of your life, but *the* blessing affects every aspect of your life. You may have *a* blessing in your life, or even many blessings. But God wants you to have *the* blessing, so you can experience His fullness in every area of your life. That is what Psalm 1 is about.

Positioned for the Blessing

The blessing is not something you work for. It is a gift from God, a matter of pure grace. You do not earn the blessing; you receive it. But in order to receive it you must be positioned properly. There are two parts to this. The first one is negative. To be positioned for the blessing, you must first dislocate yourself—remove yourself from certain influences:

> Blessed is the man
> Who walks not in the counsel of the ungodly,
>> Nor stands in the path of sinners,
>> Nor sits in the seat of the scornful.
>
>> (Psalm 1:1)

The ungodly are those who do not belong to the Lord. They do not understand His ways and have no idea how to receive His blessing. Their advice comes from the world and will always ultimately lead to failure. Do not walk in their counsel.

The path of sinners leads in the wrong direction. The word "sinner" comes from the Hebrew word *chatta*, which literally means to "miss the mark." The way of sinners will lead you astray, and if you follow it, you will end up with cursing, not blessing. Do not stand in their path.

The scornful are those who know only how to mock what is good. In Biblical terms, they are fools, and their end is destruction. Do not sit with them.

As important as it is to remove yourself from the negative influence of sinners and fools, that is not enough. You must also position yourself under the positive influence of the Word of God. That is the activity of the person who enjoys the blessing:

> But his delight is in the law of the LORD,
>> And in His law he meditates day and night.
>
>> (Psalm 1:2)

The person who is positioned for the blessing does not delight in the advice of the world. He takes no joy in the aimless way of the wicked. He has no desire for the folly of mockers. He finds his pleasure elsewhere—in the law of the Lord. The Hebrew word for "law" is *torah* and may just as well be translated "instruction." We often think of the law as judgment and condemnation, but the real purpose of *torah* is to offer life-giving instruction. It not only leads to blessing, it is itself a blessing. It becomes judgment only when our lives run counter to it.

The law of the Lord is the Word of God in all its manifestations. To delight in it is to delight in the Lord Himself, for His heart is revealed by His Word. When we honor His Word, we honor His heart. When we honor His heart, He honors ours. "Delight yourself in the LORD," the Bible says, "and He shall give you the desires of your heart" (Psalm 37:4).

What you delight in is revealed by where you spend your time. The person who delights in the LORD and in His instruction spends his time meditating on the Word of God. He thinks about it day and night. The Hebrew word for "meditate" literally means to mutter—the murmuring sound you make when you are speaking to yourself. Meditating on the law of the Lord means that you no longer speak the words of the world to yourself, but the words that come from God. As God instructed His people:

> These words which I command you today shall be in your heart. You shall talk of them when you sit in your house, when you walk by the way, when you lie down, and when you rise up. You shall bind them as a sign on your hand, and they shall be as frontlets between your eyes. You shall write them on the doorposts of your house and on your gates. (Deuteronomy 6:6-9)

That's meditation—total immersion in the Word of God!

Living in the Blessing

Now here is how the Bible describes the person who has positioned himself for blessing:

> He shall be like a tree
> Planted by the rivers of water,

> That brings forth its fruit in its season,
> Whose leaf also shall not wither;
> And whatever he does shall prosper.
>
> (Psalm 1:3)

Living in the blessing means being planted like a tree beside rivers of water. The tree symbolizes a life that is lived in wisdom, and the fruit such a life bears. To be planted means to be established, rooted, well grounded. This does not describe a tree growing randomly in the wild, but one that has been carefully cultivated.

"Rivers of water" refers to the instruction of the Lord, upon which the blessed man meditates day and night. He draws his strength and vigor from the Word of God, just as the tree draws its vitality from the rivers of water. He is well irrigated from the heart of God, and so he flourishes.

In the Old Testament, rivers of water flowed *beside* God's people. But in the New Testament, rivers of living water flow forth from *within* God's people. Jesus said, "He who believes in Me, out of his heart will flow rivers of living water" (John 7:38). He was talking about the flow of the Holy Spirit in the life the believer. The river is both the Word of God and the Spirit of God working together. For the Holy Spirit is the source of the Word, and makes the Word come alive within our own spirit.

Living in the blessing means fruitfulness. The tree of blessing is not dependent upon the variableness of the rainfall, but is always watered by the river. So it always has plenty of fruit to bear when it comes into its season. Likewise, the Word of God is constant and unchanging. When we meditate upon it, we will always have fruit to bear in season. There are seasons of growing and seasons of bearing fruit, and each fruit has its due season. Therefore, "let us not grow weary while doing good, for in due season we shall reap if we do not lose heart" (Galatians 6:9).

Fruit is the overflow of the blessing. When the river of God—

His Word and Spirit—flows through us, it shows up on our branches as fruit. Just as the fruit of an apple tree is apples, and the fruit of an orange tree is oranges, the fruit of the blessing is blessing. It multiplies blessing and conveys it to others. Just as the fruit of an apple tree contains the seeds for more apple trees, and thus for more apples, the fruit of blessing contains the seeds for more blessing.

Living in the blessing means prosperity. Those who are planted beside the rivers of God, established under His influence, will remain fresh and green. For the Word of God is unvarying, and the Holy Spirit knows no drought season. There is no withering, not even in old age. "Those who are planted in the house of the LORD shall flourish in the courts of our god. They shall still bear fruit in old age; they shall be fresh and flourishing, to declare that the LORD is upright" (Psalm 92:13-15).

When the river of God's Word and Spirit flows through you, whatever you do will prosper. To prosper means to push forward, to break out, to come mightily, to go over and excel. It is the fullness of success and abundance. The Bible says that the Lord has pleasure in the prosperity of His people (Psalm 35:27).

Our God is a God of abundance and joy, of health and prosperity, of success and fullness. Every good gift comes from Him, and no good thing will He withhold from those who have been made righteous in Jesus Christ. He has made every provision for you, in every area of your life—through the blood of Jesus, through the power of the Holy Spirit, and through the river of His Word. He is a God of blessing, and the desire of His heart is for you to live in His blessing.

God Wants You Healthy, Wealthy and Wise

"Early to bed, early to rise, makes a man healthy, wealthy and wise." This saying, attributed to Benjamin Franklin, has often been quoted, and although I can't personally vouch for its accuracy, it does bear a certain amount of common sense. However, this I *do* know, and for a certainty: It is God's will and desire for you to walk in health, prosperity and wisdom. You'll find this indicated in many places throughout Scripture, but let's consider Proverbs 3, where it is laid out all in a row: health, wealth and wisdom.

Health

God wants to bless you with health!

Do not be wise in your own eyes;
    Fear the LORD and depart from evil.
It will be health to your flesh,
    And strength to your bones.

(Proverbs 3:7-8)

"Do not be wise in your own eyes." Our eyes give us a very superficial understanding of the world. There is more to life than what our physical senses can tell us, or even what our ability to reason can show. The Bible says,

"My thoughts are not your thoughts,
  Nor are your ways My ways," says the Lord.
 "For as the heavens are higher than the earth,
  So are My ways higher than your ways,
  And My thoughts than your thoughts."

(Isaiah 55:8-9)

Wisdom does not come by what we see, or even by what we think. Paul said that we walk by faith, not by sight (2 Corinthians 5:7). This means that some things are known only by revelation—that is, God must show us.

Do not be wise in your own eyes, but "fear the Lord and depart from evil." How different God's way of wisdom is from our own. We judge externally, with our eyes. Consequently, our wisdom is shallow. But the Bible says, "The fear of the Lord is the beginning of wisdom" (Psalm 111:10). Fear of the Lord is an action of the heart and is based upon God, not on our own understanding.

To fear the Lord is to treasure His favor above all else and avoid His displeasure at all costs. It is to love what He loves and hate what He hates. It is total dependence upon Him, turning away from evil and everything that does not come from Him.

The fear of the Lord is like the breathtaking awesomeness of seeing the Grand Canyon for the first time. Or the healthy respect an electrician has for electricity, recognizing the great benefit it brings, but also aware of how risky it is to treat it lightly.

The fear of the Lord, is a pathway of healing. "It will be health to your flesh, and strength to your bones." The Hebrew word for "health" comes from the word *rapha*, which means "to heal." There is, of course, healing for the inner man—the forgiveness of sins, and release from bondages and strongholds. But God also promises healing for the body: health to the flesh and strength to the bones. The Message Bible says, "Your body will glow with health, your very bones will vibrate with life!" God wants to heal every

80

part. The flesh includes all the soft tissues and internal organs, and the bones are the structural framework. The strength of the bones is found in the marrow, which is also important to your blood system.

Jesus is our healer. Speaking of Messiah, the prophet Isaiah said, "Surely He has borne our griefs [literally "sicknesses"] and carried our sorrows [literally "pains"] ... He was wounded for our transgressions, He was bruised for our iniquities; the chastisement for our peace was upon Him, and by His stripes we are healed" (Isaiah 53:4-5).

Wealth

God wants to bless you with wealth!

Honor the LORD with your possessions,
    And with the firstfruits of all your increase;
So your barns will be filled with plenty,
    And your vats will overflow with new wine.

(Proverbs 3:9-10)

"Honor the LORD with your possessions." God wants to bless us with wealth, but first, He wants us to bless Him with our substance. The word for "honor" (Hebrew *kabad*) means "glory" and literally refers to weightiness. God's glory is the "weight" or value of His goodness.

To honor God is to glorify Him. There is a substance, or tangibility to it. It is not merely a thought or intention, but a bringing of tribute. We honor the LORD with our possessions, "and the firstfruits of all [our] increase." Increase is the fruit that has been produced or the income that has been gained.

The Bible says, "And you shall remember the LORD your God, for it is He who gives you power to get wealth, that He may establish His covenant which He swore to your fathers" (Deuteronomy 8:17). God gives us the ability to get increase and wealth because He has a promise to keep, a covenant to establish in the world. We remember Him by bringing Him our "firstfruits." This is not just *a* portion, but the *first* portion. It belongs to the Lord.

Honoring the Lord with our possessions is a pathway to abundance and prosperity. "So your barns will be filled with plenty, and your vats will overflow with new wine." A barn is a storehouse. The Hebrew word comes from a root which means "to heap together."

When we give God our first and best, He fills our storehouses, heaping them up to overflowing. It is just as Jesus said, "Give, and it will be given to you: good measure, pressed down, shaken together, and running over will be put into your bosom. For with the same measure that you use, it will be measured back to you" (Luke 6:38). Paul added, "God is able to make all grace abound toward you, that you, always having all sufficiency in all things, may have an abundance for every good work. (2 Corinthians 9:8).

The riches of our wealth come through the Lord Jesus Christ. "For you know the grace of our Lord Jesus Christ, that though He was rich, yet for your sakes He became poor, that you through His poverty might become rich" (2 Corinthians 8:9). "And my God shall supply all your need according to His riches in glory by Christ Jesus" (Philippians 4:19).

Wisdom

God wants to bless you with wisdom!

Happy is the man who finds wisdom,
    And the man who gains understanding;
For her proceeds are better than the profits of silver,
    And her gain than fine gold.
She is more precious than rubies,
    And all the things you may desire cannot compare with her.
Length of days is in her right hand,
    In her left hand riches and honor.
Her ways are ways of pleasantness,

And all her paths are peace.
She is a tree of life to those who take hold of her,
And happy are all who retain her.

(Proverbs 3:13-18)

"Happy is the man who finds wisdom." There is nothing on earth like the wisdom of God. It can do more for you than the sum of all the silver, gold and precious stones on the planet. It excels in all things. See the reward it brings:

▶ *Length of days.* This is life—long life, and full of health.

▶ *Riches and honor.* Wisdom brings forth the substance of heaven, transfusing the tangible riches of earth. This is the same kind of honor with which we honor God. When we honor Him, He honors us.

▶ *Pleasantness.* Wisdom is a pathway of beauty, delight and sweetness.

▶ *Peace.* This is the *shalom* of God—wholeness and well-being.

▶ *Tree of life.* Wisdom is life-giving, offering fruit for every season and situation.

▶ *Happiness.* The Hebrew word for "happy" is *asher*. It means to be straight, level, honest, and right; to go forward and prosper. That is what the wisdom of God causes us to do—to go forward and prosper.

"Happy is the man who finds wisdom ... Happy are all who retain her." But how do we find wisdom? And how do we retain it?

True wisdom comes from God and is imparted to us by the Holy Spirit. In Ephesians, Paul's prayer for believers was that God would give them "the spirit of wisdom and revelation in the knowledge of Him" (Ephesians 1:17).

God is happy to share His wisdom with whoever wants it—just ask! James said, "If any of you lacks wisdom, let him ask of God, who gives to all liberally and without reproach, and it will be given to him" (James 1:5). God gives His wisdom freely, no questions asked. But you have to ask in faith, for James continued, "But let him ask in faith, with no doubting, for he who doubts is like a wave of the sea driven and tossed by the wind" (v. 6)

We continue in wisdom by continuing in the fear of the LORD, by walking in His ways and depending upon Him. We continue in wisdom by faith in Jesus Christ. Paul said, "But of Him you are in Christ Jesus, who became for us wisdom from God—and righteousness and sanctification and redemption" (1 Corinthians 1:30). Stay close to Jesus and you will stay close to wisdom.

God wants you to be healthy, wealthy and wise, and He has already made provision for everything you need. The Bible says,

> Bless the LORD, O my soul,
> And forget not all His benefits:
> Who forgives all your iniquities,
> Who heals all your diseases,
> Who redeems your life from destruction,
> Who crowns you with lovingkindness and tender mercies,
> Who satisfies your mouth with good things,
> So that your youth is renewed like the eagle's.
>
> (Psalm 103:2-5)

> For the LORD God is a sun and shield;
> The LORD will give grace and glory;
> No good thing will He withhold
> From those who walk uprightly.
>
> (Psalm 84:11)

This provision is found in the Lord Jesus Christ, who said, "I have come that [you] may have life, and that [you] may have it more abundantly" (John 10:10). It is through Him that we are made righteous with God and, therefore, made eligible for every blessing and promise of God. "For He [God] made Him [Jesus] who knew no sin to be sin for us, that we might become the righteousness of God in Him" (2 Corinthians 5:21).

Father,

I thank You that Your will and desire is for me to be healthy, wealthy and wise. I thank You for the Lord Jesus Christ, who bore my sin that I might be made righteous before You. Who bore my sicknesses and pains, that I might be made healthy and whole. Who was made poor, that I might know every provision of heaven upon the earth. Who has become for me the very wisdom of God in my life. I receive Him now, by faith.

In Jesus' name, Amen.

Debt-Free Blessing

For the L<small>ORD</small> *your God will bless you just as He promised*
you; you shall lend to many nations, but you shall not
borrow; you shall reign over many nations,
but they shall not reign over you.
(Deuteronomy 15:6)

*I*n the Book of Deuteronomy, God renewed His covenant with His people. There He laid out for them what they could expect from Him and what He required of them. If they continued in His ways, they could look forward to many rich blessings. However, if they departed from the way of blessing, the only thing left was the curse (the way things were before). These blessings and cursings are presented in chapter 28. The first section (vv. 1-14) sets forth the promise of great provision, success and prosperity in every aspect of life. The rest of the chapter (vv. 15-68) paints a picture of lack, defeat and failure for those who depart from the way of blessing. The choice is powerfully summed up in Deuteronomy 30:19, "I have set before you life and death, blessing and cursing; therefore choose life."

In the midst of all this, God shows us something very powerful about what it means to be in debt. First, take a look at the blessing.

The LORD will open to you His good treasure, the heavens, to give the rain to your land in its season, and to bless all the work of your hand. You shall lend to many nations, but you shall not borrow. And the LORD will make you the head and not the tail; you shall be above only, and not beneath. (Deuteronomy 28:12-13)

The promise is that the people of God will have so much provision, they will be the lenders and not the borrowers.

Now look at the curse: "The alien who is among you shall rise higher and higher above you, and you shall come down lower and lower. He shall lend to you, but you shall not lend to him; he shall be the head, and you shall be the tail" (Deuteronomy 28:43-44). This is lack and failure so thorough that God's people have nothing at all to lend and instead must borrow just to meet their own needs.

These passages show that God takes a very negative view about debt. It is not presented as blessing. Nor is it presented as God's way of supplying His people with what He wants them to have. Debt is not a provision but a *lack* of provision. The borrower is not the head, but the tail. He is not on top of things, but "under the circumstances." He is not lifted high, but brought down low. He does not exercise authority, but has authority exercised over him by others.

God's Way of Blessing

Fast forward in the history of Israel to the time when they were coming out of exile. They departed from the ways of the Lord and ended up in Babylonian captivity for 70 years. Only a remnant returned. The Book of Nehemiah shows a group of them returning to Jerusalem to restore the walls of the city, but they are still beleaguered by the effects of the curse—they are under the oppressive burden of debt. This is not old debt from previous generations, but new debt, recently incurred. Nehemiah tells it this way:

There were also some who said, "We have mortgaged our lands and vineyards and houses, that we might buy grain because of the famine. There were also those who said, "We have borrowed money for the king's tax on our lands and vineyards. Yet now our flesh is as the flesh of our brethren, our children as their children; and indeed we are forcing our sons and our daughters to be slaves, and some of our daughters have been brought into slavery. It is not in our power to redeem them, for other men have our lands and vineyards." (Nehemiah 5:3-5)

Again we see debt presented in a very negative light. It may have looked like a blessing when they first got into it, a provision that would solve their famine problem. But now they realized that it was really a curse which led only to a greater problem. They thought they were simply mortgaging their lands and houses and vineyards to buy grain and take care of taxes. But now they saw that this had a profound effect on their sons and daughters—for they had mortgaged their future. What had first seemed like a solution was now revealed to be a slavery. They could only watch helplessly as their children were forced into servitude. They had no power to redeem them because they had mortgaged that power away to others.

That is what debt does. It enslaves. It does not give you power; it takes away the power you already have and gives it to others. The Bible says, "The rich rules over the poor, and the borrower is servant to the lender" (Proverbs 22:7). The root of the Hebrew word for "borrow" is *lavah* and means "to twine." When we borrow, we become entwined, twisted together with the lender. He now has the advantage over us and we are no longer free to do what we desire, for debt makes us his servant.

Debt is not God's way of blessing; it is the way of the world, a substitute for blessing. The blessing of the Lord means that we do not need to borrow. When we borrow we are walking outside of the blessing, getting into covenant with the world rather than looking to our covenant God to meet our needs. Going into debt is always an Ishmael, never an Isaac. It is always plan B, never plan A. It is the way of the world, not the way of the Kingdom. It is man's way of doing things, not God's.

God's way is to lead His people out of debt, not to lead them into it. The Bible says, "The blessing of the Lord makes one rich, and He adds no sorrow with it" (Proverbs 10:22). The reason debt does not belong to the blessing is because you cannot be rich and in debt at the same time, and the blessing makes one rich.

God has an anointing for His people that does not include debt. "It shall come to pass in that day that his burden shall be taken away from your shoulder, and his yoke from your neck, and the yoke will be destroyed because of the anointing oil" (Isaiah 10:27). Debt is a burden. Therefore, it does not belong to the anointing, for the anointing removes the burden and destroys the yoke.

God delivers His people out of bondage. When He called Moses to lead the children of Israel out of Egypt, the land of bondage, He said,

> And I will give this people favor in the sight of the Egyptians; and it shall be, when you go, that you shall not go empty-handed. But every woman shall ask of her neighbor, namely, of her who dwells near her house, articles of silver, articles of gold, and clothing; and you shall put them on your sons and daughters. So you shall plunder the Egyptians. (Exodus 3:21-22; this was fulfilled in Exodus 12:36)

The favor of the Lord means that He will lead us out of bondage, and we will not go out empty-handed. "He also brought them out with silver and gold, and there was none feeble among them" (Psalm 105:37).

Notice that the abundance with which the Lord led them out extended also to their sons and daughters. Instead of being enslaved breaking forth upon the earth.

One day we will have an experience of heaven that is fuller, richer and deeper. But it will be a difference only of degree, not of essence, for we are already made of heavenly stuff, born from above by the Spirit of God.

When the kingdom of God is fully revealed, heaven and earth will truly be one. In the meantime, keep looking down, for you are seated with Jesus in the heavenlies.

by the bondage of debt, as in Nehemiah 5, they were clothed with silver and gold. God's blessing goes even further: "A good man leaves an inheritance to his children's children, but the wealth of the sinner is stored up for the righteous" (Proverbs 13:22). Our children and our children's children for many generations may be affected by whether we choose to trust in God's provision or enter into debt.

There are many other passages which show that God's way of blessing is provision and not debt. For example, "The LORD is my shepherd, I shall not want" (Psalm 23:1). "He also blesses them, and they multiply greatly; and He does not let their cattle decrease" (Psalm 107:38). "He raises the poor out of the dust, and lifts the needy out of the ash heap, that He may seat him with princes" (Psalm 113:7). "Beloved, I pray that you may prosper in all things and be in health, just as your soul prospers" (3 John 2). There are many other such promises and not a speck of debt in any of them. You will not find any place in Scripture where God provides for His people by means of debt.

Debt is Not Sin, But Slavery

For all that the Bible has to say about debt, however, the language is only descriptive. God discourages borrowing, but has no outright prohibition against it. So if you are in debt, please know that no condemnation rests upon you because of it. Borrowing does not make you a sinner, although it certainly makes you a slave.

Understand, also, that there are different kinds of debt. One helpful way to think of debt is this: Debt is when your liabilities outweigh your assets; your minuses are greater than your pluses. Liabilities take money out of your pocket; assets put money into your pocket. On one hand, there is credit card and consumer debt—those are liabilities. On the other hand, there is mortgage debt and borrowing for business and investment—these are not assets in themselves, but they may *represent* assets.

There is a difference between borrowing for things that quickly fade (credit card and consumer debt) and investing in things that increase in value (houses, lands, businesses, investments). One takes away from your net worth and decreases your future spending power. The other, when used carefully, can enable you to add to your net worth, increasing your future spending power. Avoid the former at all costs; enter into the latter only after much prayer and wise counsel, and never without the peace of God resting upon you. (Ron Blue offers excellent counsel in his book, *The New Master Your Money: A Step-by-Step Plan for Gaining and Enjoying Financial Freedom.*)

Get Into the Blessing and Out of Debt

✓ Whatever your debt situation, be encouraged. God has favor, blessing, anointing and prosperity for you:

> Let them shout for joy and be glad,
> Who favor my righteous cause;
> And let them say continually,
> "Let the LORD be magnified,
> Who has pleasure in the prosperity of His servant."
>
> (Psalm 35:27)

The Bible also says, "He brings out those who are bound into prosperity" (Psalm 68:6). God wants to bring you out of the bondage of debt and release you into His wonderful prosperity. Here are some ways you can begin entering into the debt-free blessing God has already prepared for you.

Trust in the Lord.

✓ It is important to understand that you don't enter into the blessing by getting out of debt; you get out of debt by entering into the blessing. And the way you enter into the blessing is by faith.

Trust in the LORD with all your heart,
> And lean not on your own understanding;
In all your ways acknowledge Him,
> And He shall direct your paths.

(Proverbs 3:5-6)

When you trust in the Lord, He will direct your paths, and His way will lead you out of debt. Not only that, but those who put their trust in the Lord walk in the favor and the blessing of the Lord.

Let all those who put their trust in You rejoice;
> Let them ever shout for joy, because You defend them;
Let those also who love Your name
> Be joyful in You.
For You, O LORD, will bless the righteous;
> With favor You will surround them as with a shield.

(Psalm 5:11-12)

The Bible says, "Without faith it is impossible to please Him, for he who comes to God must believe that He is and that He is a rewarder of those who diligently seek Him" (Hebrews 11:6). If you will seek God diligently in faith, He will certainly reward you.

Getting into debt is never an act of faith. It takes no faith at all to go into debt—millions of people get into debt all the time without the first bit of faith in God. But it does take a vital and active faith for you to get out of debt.

Determine that you are going to repay your debts.

The wicked borrows and does not repay,
> But the righteous shows mercy and gives.

(Psalm 37:21)

Take a *faith* stance that you are going to repay your debts. God has no pleasure in those who shirk their responsibilities. It takes no faith at all to welch on a debt. In fact, it is a form of theft. But it honors God when you commit to repay, and He will help you. God

93

wants to prosper you so much so that, not only are all your debts paid off, but you have plenty more for generous giving.

> And God is able to make all grace abound toward you, that you, always having all sufficiency in all things, may have an abundance for every good work. (2 Corinthians 9:8)

Your faithfulness, or *faith-filledness*, in repaying your debts and giving generously will release the benefits of this grace into your life.

Determine that you will not go into debt anymore.

Make a qualitative decision that you will not go into debt anymore. This is a decision that is irrevocable—there is no back-up plan. It is a stance of faith. You can't believe God to get you out of debt while you are making plans to go back into it; there is nothing of faith in that. "Ask in faith, with no doubting, for he who doubts is like a wave of the sea driven and tossed by the wind. For let not that man suppose that he will receive anything from the Lord" (James 1:6-7).

Making this determination may be a hard step, for the way of debt is so deeply ingrained in us by the world, and the opportunities for it are so prevalent. Many Christians believe that debt is an unavoidable fact of life, and that in order to keep up or get ahead, you must be finance it with debt. But they have learned that from the world, not from the Lord.

The testimony of Scripture is quite the opposite: "And my God shall supply all your need according to His riches in glory in Christ Jesus" (Philippians 4:19). For God is "able to do exceedingly abundantly above all that we ask or think, according to the power that works in us" (Ephesians 3:20). Meditate on God's promises of provision and then ask Him to help you take this step of determination.

Give.

The apostle Paul said, "He who sows sparingly will reap sparingly, and he who sows bountifully will reap bountifully" (2 Corinthians

9:6). So give—as much as you can, and even more than you think
you can. Don't let debt keep you from sowing bountifully, or you
will limit the harvest.

We saw in Nehemiah 5 how the returning Jews responded to
famine and got into the slavery of debt. Now compare that with
Genesis 26 and what Isaac did when there was a famine in the
land. He was tempted to go down into Egypt, which looked prom-
ising although it was actually the land of bondage. But he decided
to follow the instruction of the Lord instead, "Live in the land of
which I shall tell you. Dwell in this land, and I will be with you and
bless you" (Genesis 26:1-3). In verse12 we find, "Then Isaac sowed
in that land, and reaped in the same year a hundredfold; and the
Lord blessed him."

In the time of famine, Isaac did not go down into the land of
bondage. Instead, he sowed his seed in the land God showed him
and reaped a hundredfold—maximum harvest! Isaac saw the blessing of God flow richly into his life. Will not God do the same for
you?

Sowing seed in time of famine and giving in time of debt takes
a strong and ready faith, but the return is magnificent. Jesus said,
"Assuredly, I say to you, there is no one who has left house or broth-
ers or sisters or father or mother or wife or children or lands, for
My sake and the gospel's, who shall not receive a hundredfold now
in this time" (Mark 10:29-30). God always honors giving, and giving always brings a return, just as sowing always brings a harvest.
That harvest will contain the answer to your debt.

Debt-Free Blessing

God's blessing is debt-free. Learn how to walk in it by faith,
determining that you are going to trust in Him alone. Honor your
commitments and faithfully repay them. Give your giving and sow
your sowing, believing God to bring you out of debt and into the

freedom of His faithful provision all the days of your life. Then you will "owe no one anything except to love one another" (Romans 13.8). That is the only debt worth having.

The Treasure of Your Heart

Keep your heart with all diligence,
for out of it spring the issues of life.
(Proverbs 4:23)

All the issues of your life spring forth from your heart. Your heart establishes the boundary lines of your life and sets the parameters of your success. The prosperity of your life—your family, your accomplishments, your finances, even your health—depends upon the prosperity of your heart. "Beloved, I pray that you may prosper in all things and be in health, just as your soul prospers" (3 John 2).

Your heart is the treasure house of your soul. Whatever you deposit there becomes a resource for your thoughts, your emotions and your decisions. All the issues of your life pass through your heart. So be careful what you place in it and what you allow to be at home there. Guard your heart and protect it from every danger—the course of your life depends upon it.

Watch over the words of your heart, for they are very important. The proper use of words is to convey faith and the power of God. When God wanted to create the heavens and the earth, He did it with words. Jesus calmed the wind and the waves with words, and taught His disciples to move mountains with faith-filled words. The Bible says, "Death and life are in the power of the tongue, and those who love it will eat its fruit" (Proverbs 18:21).

Such is the power of words. Keep your heart by paying close attention to the words you allow to come into it, but also by the words you allow to flow out of it.

The Word of God

The psalm writer said, "Your Word have I treasured in my heart, that I may not sin against You" (Psalm 119:11 NASB). When we allow the Word of God to be deposited in our heart, and we give it the highest priority in our life, it will keep us in right relationship with God.

The Word of God is His heart expressing itself to our hearts. But it not only reveals *His* heart, it reveals *ours* as well. "For the Word of God is living and powerful, and sharper than any two-edged sword, piercing even to the division of soul and spirit, and of joints and marrow, and is a discerner of the thoughts and intents of the heart" (Hebrews 4:12).

We treasure the Word of God by meditating on it—keeping it in our ears, fixing our eyes upon it, reflecting carefully on it, setting it in the throne room of our hearts. When we do, it brings forth a flow of wisdom and well-being into our lives.

> My son, give attention to my words;
> > Incline your ear to my saying.
> Do not let them depart from your eyes;
> > Keep them in the midst of your heart;
> For they are life to those who find them,
> > And health to all their flesh.
> Keep your heart with all diligence,
> > For out of it spring the issues of life."
>
> (Proverbs 4:20-23)

According to Psalm 19:7-11, the Word of God converts the soul, bringing positive change into your life. It makes the simple man wise. It causes the heart to rejoice. It enlightens the understanding. It is a sure foundation that strengthens our endurance. It instructs the heart in the truth and prosperity of God's ways. More precious than gold and sweeter than honey, the Word of God keeps us from harmful ways and leads us into all the good things of God.

The Words of Your Mouth

The Word of God reveals the treasure of your heart, but so do your own words. Jesus said, "A good man out of the good treasure of his heart brings forth good; and an evil man out of the evil treasure brings forth evil. For out of the abundance of the heart his mouth speaks" (Luke 6:46).

Whether the treasure of your heart is good or bad, your words will show it. This is especially true when you find yourself in difficult situations—pressure can be a great diagnostic.

But it is not simply a matter of what is in your heart, it is what is in your heart *in abundance* that counts. For that is what comes out of your mouth, especially at the critical points of your life. If the Word of God is in your heart in abundance, then the words of your mouth will be in agreement with it. This is a very powerful thing because the Bible says that God's Word will not return to Him void, but will accomplish His will and prosper in whatever He sends it to do (Isaiah 55:11). God's Word in your mouth, when you speak it in faith, is every bit as powerful as God's Word in His mouth. When the treasure of God's Word is in your heart and goes forth from your mouth, it brings God's prosperity into your life.

Being careful about what you say is a key element to keeping your heart from danger. "Keep your heart with all diligence, for out of it spring the issues of life. Put away from you a deceitful mouth, and put perverse lips far from you" (Proverbs 4:23-24). A

99

deceitful mouth twists and distorts things. It does not tell the truth and cannot be trusted.

A perverse mouth speaks words that we do not really mean to say. How often we speak without thinking, saying things we do not mean, uttering words we would not want to come true. But we are responsible for them anyway! Jesus said, "But I say to you that for every idle word men may speak, they will give account of it in the day of judgment. For by your words you will be justified, and by your words you will be condemned" (Matthew 12:36-37). Idle words are a symptom of a heart that is not yet overflowing with God's Word. They have no faith to them, nor do they accomplish what God desires to perform in our lives.

This connection between the heart and the mouth is very important. It is foundational to our experience, even to our salvation. The Bible says:

> But what does it say? "The word is near you, in your mouth and in your heart" (that is, the word of faith which we preach): that if you confess with your mouth the Lord Jesus and believe in your heart that God has raised Him from the dead, you will be saved. For with the heart one believes unto righteousness, and with the mouth confession is made unto salvation. (Romans 10:8-10)

We believe with the heart; we confess with the mouth. Both are important, for out of the overflow of the heart, the mouth speaks. Both are required, because God speaks His Word to the world *through* His people. "For prophecy never came by the will of man, but holy men of God spoke as they were moved by the Holy Spirit" (2 Peter 1:21).

No wonder David prayed, "Let the words of my mouth and the meditation of my heart be acceptable in Your sight, O LORD, my strength and my Redeemer"(Psalm 19:14). "Who is the man who desires life and loves many days, that he may see good? Keep your tongue from evil, and your lips from speaking lies" (Psalm 34:12-13). "Set a guard, O LORD, over my mouth; keep watch over the door of my lips" (Psalm 141:3).

Keeping Your Heart

The Word of God is a very great treasure indeed! If you will carefully cultivate it in your heart and consistently express it with the words of your mouth, you will see the blessing and prosperity of God abound in your life. "Keep your heart with all diligence, for out of it spring the issues of life."

Dear Lord,

Thank You for Your life-changing Word. It gives me wisdom and understanding. It instructs me in the way I should go and causes my heart to rejoice. Your Word is precious to me, and sweet.

I treasure Your Word in my heart, that I might not sin against You. Your Word is a lamp for my feet and a light for my path, and I am preserved by paying attention to it.

Father, out of the overflow of my heart my mouth speaks. Fill my heart with Your Word, that I may have a good treasure to bring forth by my speech. Set a guard, O LORD, over my mouth. Keep watch over the door of my lips, that the words of my mouth and the meditation of my heart may be pleasing in Your sight, O LORD, my Strength and my Redeemer.

In Jesus' name, Amen.

Where Your Treasure Is

Where Your treasure is, there your heart will be also.
(Matthew 6:21)

*L*et's put it bluntly: What you treasure in your heart is revealed by how you handle money. What is your attitude toward it? Jesus said, "You cannot serve God and mammon" (Matthew 6:24). This does not mean you cannot have money, simply that you cannot serve it. Money can be your servant, but not your master. That is the context in which Jesus spoke the following words:

> Do not lay up for yourselves treasures on earth, where moth and rust destroy and where thieves break in and steal; but lay up for yourselves treasures in heaven, where neither moth nor rust destroys and where thieves do not break in and steal. For where your treasure is, there your heart will be also. (Matthew 6:19-21)

This calls for a change of heart. Stop depositing your treasure on earth—that is the force of "do not lay up for yourselves"—stop doing it! Start making your deposits in heaven. Begin thinking about your life, your resources, your money, in a new way. You are an agent of heaven, for the kingdom of heaven is now breaking forth in the world, and God calls us to seek after it. Jesus said,

Therefore do not worry, saying, "What shall we eat?" or "What shall we drink?" or "What shall we wear?" For after all these things the Gentiles seek. For your heavenly Father knows that you need all these things. But seek first the kingdom of God and His righteousness, and all these things shall be added to you. (Matthew 6:31-33)

The kingdom of God is His rule and reign, in heaven and on earth. The righteousness of God is His way to being and doing right—it is His "rightness." These are the things we are to seek now. When we do, everything else will be taken care of. This is banking on heaven. It is why Jesus said, "Don't worry about tomorrow, tomorrow will take care of itself" (Matthew 6:34, my paraphrase).

Seated in the Heavenlies

The Bible says that we are seated in the heavenlies in Christ Jesus (Ephesians 2:6). Notice the tense. It does not say that we *will be* seated in the heavenlies, but that we *are* seated there—right now! Therefore, get the perspective of heaven on your life and resources. When you make a deposit of them in heaven, they are blessed, empowered with the substance of heaven. In that way, they become truly useful to you, even in this life.

Jesus taught us to pray, "Your will be done on earth as it is in heaven" (Matthew 6.10). That is supposed to happen with our treasure as much as with anything else in our lives. That is why we need our treasure to be blessed with the purposes of heaven, so it can be used for God's kingdom on the earth.

The Scent of Heaven

Our hearts are to be so focused on heaven, where we are seated, that our lives—and our money—naturally begin to manifest the scent, the savor and the substance of heaven upon the earth. This is not just a matter of tithing to the church or giving to charity.

Those are good and proper things, and we ought to do them. But laying up treasures in heaven is about much more than that. It is about depositing our whole lives—*everything*—in the bank of heaven, and that requires a basic re-orientation of the heart. Or else we might end up like the man Jesus spoke about in this parable:

> The ground of a certain rich man yielded plentifully. And he thought within himself, saying, "What shall I do, since I have no room to store my crops?"
>
> So he said, "I will do this: I will pull down my barns and build greater, and there I will store all my crops and my goods. And I will say to my soul, 'Soul, you have many goods laid up for many years; take your ease; eat, drink, and be merry.'"
>
> But God said to him, "Fool! This night your soul will be required of you; then whose will those things be which you have provided?"
>
> So is he who lays up treasure for himself, and is not rich toward God (Luke 12:16-21).

This man was rich, and on the increase, but he lacked the proper perspective. He thought it was all about him—he had an "I" problem. He didn't realize that he was blessed to be a blessing. He was not hooked up to God's way of being and doing, and when he died, his treasure had no lasting value.

Consider the rich young ruler, another man who had the same problem:

> Jesus said to him, "If you want to be perfect, go, sell what you have and give to the poor, and you will have treasure in heaven; and come, follow Me." But when the young man heard that saying, he went away sorrowful, for he had great possessions. (Matthew 19:21-22)

This young man thought he wanted the things of heaven, but it turned out that he was actually more focused on the things of the earth. He was trying to serve both God and his own possessions.

He was a double-minded man, unstable in all his ways. He might have experienced the joy of God's way of being and doing, for the kingdom of God is about "righteousness and peace and joy in the Holy Spirit" (Romans 14:17). Instead, he went away sorrowful. He held onto his possessions and they never radiated with the savor of heaven. They never blessed anyone with the power and love of God.

All That We Have

Now, here is another man whose heart was completely different. We catch a brief glimpse of him in one of the parables Jesus told:

> The kingdom of heaven is like treasure hidden in a field, which a man found and hid; and for joy over it he goes and sells all that he has and buys that field. (Matthew 13:45)

Do you see where his heart is? It is in that treasure. Somehow, he has stumbled across the kingdom of God, and it fills him with such joy that he takes everything he has and buys that field, just so he can possess that treasure. All his possessions have now been converted to the substance of the kingdom. Everything in his life now takes on the smell and taste of heaven, and he begins to go forth as a son of the kingdom to fulfill the destiny for which he was created. He has become a world-changer.

Paul was talking to people just like this man when he said, "My God shall supply all your need according to His riches in glory by Christ Jesus" (Philippians 4:19). The Philippian believers, to whom Paul was writing, decided that they were going to be partners with what God was doing in the world. That is what they treasured in their hearts. Their money, and everything else in their lives simply followed. And God supplied all their need.

Paul challenged the believers at Corinth with how the believers at Macedonia laid up treasures in heaven. Even in a time of great affliction and deep poverty, the Macedonians gave of themselves sacrificially, and quite generously.

> For I bear witness that according to their ability, yes, and beyond their ability, they were freely willing, imploring us with much urgency that we would receive the gift and the fellowship of the ministering to the saints. And not only as we had hoped, but they first gave themselves to the Lord, and then to us by the will of God. (2 Corinthians 8:3-5)

Do you see where their heart was? Did you notice the secret of their openhandedness? *They first gave themselves to the Lord.* They were seeking His rule and reign in their lives. They were pursuing His way of being and doing. After that, giving themselves to others was a natural outflow of the power and love of God at work in them. Their heart was simply the conduit.

That is the kind of heart God treasures, and this is how He responds to it: "God is able to make all grace abound toward you, that you, always having all sufficiency in all things, may have an abundance for every good work" (2 Corinthians 9:8).

In Everything You Do

Please understand, I do not write this so that you will learn merely to give more, although I believe that if you understand what I am saying, you will indeed find yourself giving more and more. Rather, I write so that, *whatever* you do with your time, your talents, your treasure, your life, you will do it as one who passionately seeks after God's rule and reign in the world, to learn His way of being and doing.

This will have far-reaching effects and will show up in ways large and small. It will appear, not only in how you give to church and charity, but also in how you pay your bills. When your heart is in heaven, and heaven is in your heart, your money is blessed.

Even a little thing like writing a check to the electric company becomes an act of godliness that adds to the prosperity of God's kingdom. It honors God because God pays His bills (and when you lay up your treasure in heaven, your bills become His bills).

The treasure of your heart will show up even in how well you tip. Imagine what would happen if Christians really got a strong hold of this. Waiters and waitresses would no longer dread the Sunday lunchtime church crowd because they would no longer be getting stiffed! Sundays would become a joy to them, and it could possibly be the birth of a revival movement among restaurant folk. It would be the will of God being done on earth as it is in heaven, for God so loves that He gives.

A New Perspective

Lay up for yourselves treasures in heaven, for that is where you are now seated. It is where you operate from in the rule and reign of God. Let the perspective of heaven now come forth in all that you have and in everything you do. Let it radiate with the power and love of God overflowing in your life. In this way, your treasure will have lasting value and you will fulfill your destiny to be a world-changer. For wherever your treasure is, that is where your heart is also.

How to be a Hilarious Giver

So let each one give as he purposes in his heart,
not grudgingly or of necessity;
for God loves a cheerful giver.
(2 Corinthians 9:7)

Paul said that God loves a cheerful giver. The Greek word for "cheerful" is *hilaros*, which is, of course, where we get our English word "hilarious." Now, this doesn't mean that you must be boisterous or convulsive, rolling on the floor in laughter at offering time (although, don't be surprised if God hits you with that manifestation someday when you least expect it). But it does mean that God wants you to understand and experience giving as a very positive, joy-filled thing. A heart that is not only willing and able, but full of grace and gladness at the prospect of giving, is a heart that is coming into line with the heart of God. That is why Paul said,

> But as you abound in everything—in faith, in speech, in knowledge, in all diligence, and in your love for us—see that you abound in this grace [giving] also. (2 Corinthians 8:7)

Supernatural faith, divine utterance and revelation knowledge are wonderful gifts from the Spirit of God. To be diligent and love with the love that comes from God is very important. But just as wonderful and important is the act of giving. It is a divine grace, and when you let the Holy Spirit develop this grace in your life, the joy you experience is the joy of God Himself.

How *Not* To Be a Hilarious Giver

There are plenty of grumpy givers in the Church, more than enough to go around. These are the ones who, when the pastor is exhorting them about giving, fold their arms, cross their legs and turn their bodies toward the side of the pew. They think of the offering as a duty, an obligation, a "temple tax" that must be paid so God doesn't get mad at them. Some think that they are just "paying their way," and if God is having a blessed day, they might even leave Him a tip. They make it all about themselves and not about God. Here is how to become a grumpy giver:

▸ *Give sparingly.* Then you will experience the dryness of reaping sparingly. For as you sow, that is how you will reap.

▸ *Give grudgingly.* Not out of a generous spirit, but out of a tight and bitter heart.

▸ *Give out of necessity.* Because you think you need to score points with God, with others or with the IRS.

How *To* Be a Hilarious Giver

If you would rather be a hilarious giver than a grumpy one, here are some important things to remember that will help you get started.

First, give yourself to the LORD
Consider the vibrant faith of the Macedonian Christians:

Moreover, brethren, we make known to you the grace of God bestowed on the churches of Macedonia; that in a great trail of affliction the abundance of their joy and their deep poverty abounded in the riches of their liberality. For I bear witness that according to their ability, yes, and beyond their ability, they were freely willing, imploring us with much urgency that we would receive the gift and the fellowship of the ministering to the saints. And not only as we had hoped, but *they first gave themselves to the Lord*, and then to us by the will of God. (2 Corinthians 8:1-5)

Even in the midst of great affliction and deep poverty, these Macedonian believers were able to give far beyond their means, and with great joy. Why? Because they first gave themselves to the Lord. Giving is, first of all, a matter of the heart. John wrote, "Beloved, I pray that you may prosper in all things and be in health, just as your soul prospers" (3 John 2). It is the inward disposition of a person that determines their outward character. The Macedonian Christians had such deep and abiding joy and generosity because they had lined their hearts up with the heart of God and committed themselves to His desires. So great was their desire, they were actually *begging* to be a part of what God was doing. They understood that it was not about them, but all about Him.

Second, purpose in your heart

When you give yourself to the Lord, the purpose of your heart becomes established. So get into your relationship with the Father. Set your love on Him and listen for His voice. He will show you what to do. Don't wait until the last minute to determine what or how you will give. Plan ahead, then when the time for giving comes, you will be excited about bringing your offering to Him. It may sound paradoxical, but you can also plan for some spontaneous giving. Purpose in your heart that you are going to be a giver.

Next, remember the law of the harvest

Paul said, "He who sows sparingly will also reap sparingly, and he who sows bountifully will also reap bountifully" (2 Corinthians

9:6). When you hold back on your sowing, you are also holding back on your harvest. But when you sow bountifully (literally, "with blessings"), you will also reap bountifully (with blessings). Jesus said:

> Give, and it will be given to you: good measure, pressed down, shaken together, and running over will be put into your bosom. For with the same measure that you use, it will be measured back to you. (Luke 6:38-9)

> Assuredly, I say to you, there is no one who has left house or brothers or sisters or father or mother or wife or children or lands, for My sake and the gospel's, who shall not receive a hundredfold now in this time—houses and brothers and sisters and mothers and children and lands, with persecutions—and in the age to come, eternal life. (Mark 10:29-30)

Get on the bountiful side of giving and you will experience the joy of a harvest that is rich with blessings.

Then, focus on the ability and favor of God

One reason some Christians are grumpy givers is because they think they will come up short if they give away too much of their resources. But Paul said, "God is able to make all grace abound toward you, that you, always having all sufficiency in all things, may have an abundance for every good work" (2 Corinthians 9:8). Notice the superlatives: *all* grace, *always*, *all* sufficiency in *all* things. This is not *just* enough, but *more than* enough. It is overflow, so that you may also have something with which to bless others. This means that you can give freely, confident that you will not come up short.

> Honor the LORD with your possessions,
>   And with the firstfruits of all your increase;
> So you barns will be filled with plenty,
>   And your vats overflow with new wine.
>
> (Proverbs 3:9-10)

Honor the Lord with your firstfruits—the first and the best, not the last and the least. Sow honor, and you will reap honor. Sow the first and the best, and you will reap the first and the best. Your barns will be filled, piled high with plenty, and your vats will overflow with fresh wine. That is, you will have all you need, and more—and it will be the good stuff! God has promised this for those who honor and obey Him: "The LORD will command the blessing on you in your storehouses and in all to which you set your hand" (Deuteronomy 28:8).

Consider the blessing Paul offered for the hilarious giver:

Now He who supplies seed to the sower, and bread for food, supply and multiply the seed you have sown and increase the fruits of your righteousness, while you are enriched in everything for all liberality, which causes thanksgiving through us to God. (2 Corinthians 9:10-11)

Our God is the God of increase and abundance. His grace is so rich that, if you desire to sow, He will supply you with the seed. Then when you sow it, He will multiply that seed and increase the harvest that comes from your giving. The result is that you will be enriched in *everything* and have plenty more for all kinds of generosity—a never-ending circle of blessing. That is certainly something to be joyful about.

A Joyful Tither

Let's talk about the tithe. It is a special form of giving by which God desires for us to honor Him, and by which He also desires to honor us. The tithe is the tenth—not just *a* tenth, but *the* tenth. That is, it is the *first* tenth. It is the first and the best, not the last and the least. When we give the first tenth of our increase to the Lord, we are recognizing and honoring Him as the source of our supply and of all that is good in our lives. When we give the tithe,

God not only honors and blesses the tenth, but He honors and blesses the other ninety per cent as well.

Under the Law of Moses, Israel was required to tithe. It was not a free-will option, but a covenant obligation. That is why God declares, in Malachi 3:8, that Israel had robbed Him in tithes and offerings—they did not fulfill their part of the bargain.

But before the Mosaic Law, tithing was a free-will offering. Abraham, for example, freely gave a tenth of his increase (the spoils he had won from his recent battle) to Melchizedek, God's priest (Genesis 14:18-20). At Bethel, Jacob made a vow to God, "Of all that You give me I will surely give a tenth to You" (Genesis 28:22). These were not obligations of any law or regulation, but offerings made from the heart.

For the children of God under the new and better covenant mediated by Jesus Christ, there is no longer any legal obligation to tithe. No penalty attaches to us if we fail to give the tenth to the LORD. No atonement is necessary. The only obligation for Christians is the continuing debt to love one another: "Owe no one anything except to love one another, for he who loves another has fulfilled the law" (Romans 13:8). All the Law and the prophets, Jesus said, hang on these two things: Love the Lord your God with all your heart, with all your soul, and with all your mind, and love your neighbor as yourself (Matthew 22:37-40).

On the other hand, there is a tremendous benefit and blessing in tithing. In Malachi 3, God gives us this challenge, with great promise:

> "Bring all the tithes into the storehouse,
>   That there may be food in My house,
> And try Me in this,"
>   Says the LORD of Hosts,
> "If I will not open for you the windows of heaven
>   And I will pour out for you such a blessing

That there will not be room enough to receive it.
And I will rebuke the devourer for your sakes,
    So that he will not destroy the fruit of your ground,
Nor shall the vine fail to bear fruit for you in the field."
    Says the LORD of Hosts;
"And all the nations will call you blessed,
    For you will be a delightful land,"
    Says the LORD of Hosts.

(Malachi 3:10-12)

This is the only place in Scripture where God invites us to test Him. It is a matter of faith, which greatly pleases God, and the reward is three-fold:

> ▸ God promises to open the windows of heaven and pour out such a blessing on us that there will not be enough room to receive it. He will empty out heaven on our behalf, holding nothing back. This is not just sufficiency, but superabundance. Our biggest problem will then be what to do with it all!

> ▸ God promises that He Himself will rebuke the devourer for us. This second promise is as great as the first. It means that the great blessing we receive will not be dissipated, eaten away, stolen by the enemy or otherwise go to waste. We will bear our fruit in season. It will not be cast early and spoiled, but will come to maturity for a full and bountiful harvest.

> ▸ God promises us a delightful land—a land full of delight, and very desirable. The nations will see our prosperity and acknowledge that we are blessed. And it will be a glory to God.

Giving the tithe to the Lord is no longer the duty of law but the prerogative of love. It is not about religion, but about relationship.

It is not a legal obligation that is laid upon us but a gracious opportunity that is set before us. It is the joy of knowing Him intimately, experiencing His love flowing through us, participating with Him in His plan to bless and redeem the world, and seeing the abundance of His provision come forth richly. This is the joy of the hilarious giver.

How to Encourage Yourself in the LORD

David encouraged himself in the LORD his God.
(1 Samuel 30:6 KJV)

$\mathcal{D}$avid and his band of soldiers had just returned home to Ziklag, only to find that it had been burned with fire, and their wives and children carried off by the Amalekites. "Discouraged" is not a big enough word to describe the state of their morale. The Bible says that they wept bitter tears until they simply had no more power to weep. For David, it was even worse, for he was their leader, and his men were so consumed by grief that there was even talk of stoning him. He was in distress, and it might have destroyed him completely, except for this: David encouraged himself in the LORD his God.

This required a definite resolve on David's part, an act of his volition. To default on this decision would only have deepened his distress, and discouragement would have rendered him helpless. What is more, the wives and children of him and his men would have been lost forever.

So David chose encouragement, not only to *be* encouraged — for there was no one around him who could, or would, do that for him — but to encourage *himself*. The most important thing to notice here, though, is that David did not encourage himself in himself. Rather, the Scripture says that he encouraged himself *in the* LORD *his God.* You see, this was not just about David, for David had a covenant with God, and that made this whole thing God's business. Having thus encouraged himself, David was then able to move on to the solution God had prepared for this problem.

Understanding Discouragement

Before we go on and talk about encouragement, there are a couple of things we need to understand about discouragement. First, discouragement does not come from the Lord; it comes from our adversary the devil. He wants us to loose heart and quit, so he looks for every opportunity to whisper lies and accusations in our ears. The reason David could encourage himself in the Lord was because the Lord was the source of his solution, not the source of his problem.

Second, discouragement is an indication that we are walking by sight, not by faith. Paul said, "We walk by faith, not by sight" (2 Corinthians 5:7), and that was the source of his stability and strength. When we walk by faith, with our confidence in the Lord and his promises, it is impossible to be discouraged. But when we walk by sight, trusting in our senses, our feelings and our own understanding, we easily fall prey to all the deceptions of the world, the flesh and the devil. When we find ourselves in discouragement, we discover where we have been placing our trust. The solution is to put our trust back in the Lord.

Paul said that faith comes by hearing, and hearing by the Word of God (Romans 10:17). So when discouragement comes and you find that you have been walking by sight instead of by faith, head back to the Scriptures and let the promises of God build your faith back up to strength.

God Wants You to be Encouraged

God wants you to be encouraged and He has given you the means by which you can encourage yourself in Him.

First, recognize that you do not have to stay discouraged. Discouragement may fly over your head like a bird, but you do not have to let it nest in your hair. You can be encouraged, and in fact, you can encourage yourself.

Second, remember that, if you know the Lord Jesus Christ, you are in covenant with God, and He has committed Himself to take care of you in every situation. When the circumstances of life pressed in on David, David pressed in on the benefits of his covenant relationship with God. He briefly outlined these in Psalm 103.

Bless the LORD, O my soul,
and forget not all His benefits:
Who forgives all your iniquities,
Who heals all your diseases,
Who redeems your life from destruction,
Who crowns you with lovingkindness and tender mercies,
Who satisfies your mouth with good things,
So that your youth is renewed like the eagle's.

(Psalm 103:2-5)

Third, stop giving voice to your discouragement and start giving voice to your encouragement. Stop repeating the lies of the devil and start speaking the promises of God. Stop speaking out of fear and start speaking in faith. Stop talking about the problems and start talking about the solution. Find out what the Word of God has to say about your situation, then start speaking it, rather than your feelings.

Fourth, meditate on the Lord. One of the Hebrew words for "meditate" literally means to murmur, and implies the moving of the lips. Another word means to converse with yourself. It is your "self-talk," the way you speak to yourself about the things in your life. Everybody meditates on something, but often it is on the wrong thing, on the wrong person, or with the wrong focus.

Meditation is not a matter of positive thinking, and neither is encouragement. Both are matters of faith. It is not about us, but about Him. So let your meditation be about the Lord, about His love, His Word, His promises, His goodness, His works. As you do, you will be able to cast your cares on the Lord, with strong confidence that He cares about everything going on in your life (1 Peter 5:7).

> We have thought, O God, on Your lovingkindness, in the midst of Your temple. (Psalm 48:9)

> But I will sing of Your power; yes, I will sing aloud of Your mercy in the morning; for You have been my defense and refuge in the day of my trouble. (Psalm 59:16)

> I call to remembrance my song in the night; I meditate within my heart, and my spirit makes diligent search. (Psalm 77:6)

> I will remember the works of the LORD; surely I will remember Your wonders of old. I will also meditate on all Your work, and talk of Your deeds. (Psalm 77:11-12)

> May my meditation be sweet to Him; I will be glad in the LORD. (Psalm 104:34)

> I will meditate on Your precepts, and contemplate Your ways. I will delight myself in Your statutes; I will not forget Your Word. (Psalm 119:15-16)

> Oh, how I love Your law! It is my meditation all the day. (Psalm 119:97)

> My eyes are awake through the night watches, that I may meditate on Your Word. (Psalm 119:148)

I remember the days of old; I meditate on all Your works; I muse on the work of Your hands. (Psalm 143:5)

I will meditate on the glorious splendor of Your majesty, and on Your wondrous works. (Psalm 145:5)

Fifth, get in the presence of the Lord. "Give thanks to the Lord. Enter his gates with thanksgiving and His courts with praise" (Psalm 104:4). This requires a quality decision: I will give thanks. I will praise.

Nehemiah said, "The joy of the Lord is your strength" (Nehemiah 8:10). David said to the Lord, "In Your presence is fullness of joy" (Psalm 16:11). When we get into the presence of the Lord we will find all the strength we need and encouragement for every circumstance.

Sixth, stand in the armor of God. Paul said, "Put on the whole armor of God, that you may be able to stand against the wiles of the devil." You can find a description of this in Ephesians 6.11-18:

▸ We have the truth of God's Word, the righteousness of Christ and the gospel of peace (wholeness) at work on our behalf.

▸ We have the helmet of salvation (salvation, healing, deliverance, prosperity and preservation) to guide and direct our thoughts.

▸ We have the shield of faith to quench the fiery darts of the adversary. Make no mistake, discouragement is most certainly one of the devil's fiery darts.

▸ We have the sword of the Spirit, which is the Word of God. This is the offensive weapon that silences the voice of discouragement and all the lies of the devil.

▸ We have all kinds of prayer in the Holy Spirit by which we can persevere and supply every need of the saints. Learn to pray as the Spirit of God leads.

Discouragement will tell you that you have nothing going for you and everything going against you. Encouragement tells you that you have everything going for you and that it doesn't matter what you have going against you. God is on your side, with the provision for every need and the answer for every problem you may have. That is why Jesus came, and why, like David, you can encourage yourself in the LORD your God.

Praying With Expectation

In the morning, O Lord, *you hear my voice.*
In the morning I lay my requests before
you and wait in expectation.
(Psalm 5:3 NIV)

Whenever you pray, pray with expectation. That's what David, the psalm writer, did. He had a need, he had a prayer, and he had an expectation. The NKJV says it this way: "My voice You shall hear in the morning, O Lord in the morning I will direct it to You. And I will look up."

When need arose in his life, David laid out his requests in prayer and looked to the Lord in expectation. This was not the outward directing of his physical eyes, but the inward disposition of his heart—to be ready for the readiness of God.

Centuries later, the Lord Jesus, who is called Son of David, epitomized this disposition of the heart in His own life and ministry. He continually looked to the Father in everything He did. Whenever He prayed, He always expected to receive the answer. What is more, He taught His disciples to do the same.

The Expectation of Jesus

Whatever things you ask when you pray, believe that you receive them, and you will have them. (Mark 11:24; The NIV says, "believe that you *have* received them")

Jesus' teaching is clear: When you pray, expecting that you have received, you will have whatever you ask. In another place He said:

Ask, and it will be given you; seek, and you will find; knock, and it will be opened to you. For everyone who asks receives, and he who seeks finds, and to him who knocks it will be opened. Or what man is there among you who, if his sons asks for bread, will give him a stone? Or if he asks for a fish, will he give him a serpent? If you then, being evil, know how to give good things to your children, how much more will your Father who is in heaven give good things to those who ask Him! (Matthew 7:7-11)

When you ask, expect to receive. When you seek, expect to find. When you knock, expect the door to be opened. The reason for this is that, if we know the Lord Jesus Christ, we now have God as our heavenly Father, and He is a giver of good gifts. He won't give us something bad and try to make us think it is something good. God is a good Father, and good fathers don't do that. God will give what we ask, so ask with expectation.

This kind of expectation arises out of a proper orientation of the heart, focusing ourselves on the Lord. Jesus said,

If you abide in Me, and My words abide in you, you will ask what you desire, and it shall be done for you. (John 15:7)

You did not choose Me, but I chose you and appointed you that you should go and bear fruit, and that your fruit should remain, that whatever you ask the Father in My name He may give you. (John 15:16)

> Most assuredly, I say to you, whatever you ask the Father in My
> name He will give you. Until now you have asked nothing in My
> name. Ask, and you will receive, that your joy may be full. (John
> 16:23-24)

You see, this is all about Jesus—abiding in *Him*, being chosen
and appointed by *Him*, asking the Father in *His* name. If it were all
about us, our prospects would be limited and doubtful, and our
heart would accuse us: "You're not worthy." But because it is all
about Jesus, we can expect to walk in His joy, experience His fruitfulness, and have our prayers answered just as His were answered—
because *He* is worthy!

James, the brother of Jesus, also taught about expectancy in
prayer. When we look at his epistle, we can see four types or levels
of expectation: no expectation, wrong expectation, double-minded
expectation, and single-minded expectation.

Praying with No Expectation

> Where do wars and fights come from among you? Do they not
> come from your desires for pleasure that war in you members?
> You lust and do not have. You murder and covet and cannot ob-
> tain. You fight and war. Yet you do not have because you do not
> ask. (James 4:1-2)

Certainly, this reveals a lack of expectation. Many Christians
do not have because they do not ask, and they do not ask because
they do not have an expectation of receiving. So they go looking
for their answers in all the wrong places.

We need to pray with expectation, or else there is no point in
praying at all. There are many people who pray without having
any expectation of receiving. So they receive exactly what they expect—nothing! Then they shrug their shoulders and say, "Well, you
never know what God is going to do." Prayer becomes less and less

of a resource in their lives, not because they tried it and found it lacking, but because they never *really* tried it in the first place. The problem is that they either do not know, or else do not believe what God has said in His Word, for He has said *many* things about what He is going to do. This means that we *can* know what God is going to do—He is going to keep His Word! So find out what God's Word has to say, then pray with the expectation that He is going to do it.

Praying with Wrong Expectation

> You ask and do not receive, because you ask amiss, that you may spend it on your pleasures. (James 4:3)

Some Christians, even when they do ask, still do not receive because they ask with the wrong motivation. Their expectation is twisted because they have made it all about themselves instead of about Jesus.

Jesus taught us to ask in His name, but many Christians use "in Jesus' name" as nothing more than a tagline at the end of their prayers, as if it were some sort of magic phrase. Praying in Jesus' name is not about magic but about authority, the authority we have in Jesus. Jesus gave us this authority so we could see His purpose fulfilled and His work done on the earth, just as it is in heaven. To ask in Jesus' name is to ask as *He* would ask. When we do, we can expect to receive the answer to our prayers, just as Jesus received the answer to His.

Praying with Double-Minded Expectation

> If any of you lacks wisdom, let him ask of God, who gives to all liberally and without reproach, and it will be given to him. But let him ask in faith, with no doubting, for he who doubts is like a wave of the sea driven and tossed by the wind. For let not that

man suppose that he will receive anything from the Lord; he is a double-minded man, unstable in all his ways. (James 1:5-8)

This describes the prayer of double-minded expectation because it is offered by a double-minded man. The double-minded man is confused in his expectations. He asks with the expectation that he will receive—but he also asks with doubt, the expectation that he might be denied. No wonder he is unstable in all his ways! His prayer is so confused and self-contradictory, how could God ever answer it? It makes no sense.

What the double-minded man really needs to do is press into the stability of God by getting into the Word of God, where faith comes and doubt leaves. Then his expectation will become strong and focused, and he will be confident in his prayer.

Praying with Single-Minded Expectation

Finally, James talked about praying with single-minded expectation—the prayer of faith.

Is anyone among you sick? Let him call for the elders of the church, and let them pray over him, anointing him with oil in the name of the Lord. And the prayer of faith will save the sick, and the Lord will raise him up. (James 5:14-15)

The prayer of faith is a prayer of expectation, single-minded and focused on God. It is based on the promise of God and, therefore, looks for that promise to be fulfilled. In this instance, the promise is for healing, so we can be confident in God when we pray for healing. But God has promised us many other things for which we may confidently pray. The promise of God is whatever He says He will do. In other words, it is the will of God.

Now, the will of God is not some vague thing, obscure and unknowable. It is clear and knowable, and is revealed to us in the Word of God. The Bible says that "faith comes by hearing, and hearing by the Word of God" (Romans 10:17). When we hear the Word of God, we begin to discover the will of God. As we do, faith starts to rise up within. When we exercise that faith and start taking God at His Word, our expectation grows strong, and we know that we will have whatever we ask in prayer.

Developing Your Expectation in Prayer

Here are five things you can do which will help you develop your expectation when you pray, so you can see your prayers answered.

▶ Spend time in the Word of God. Abide in it and let it abide in you. Faith comes by hearing and hearing by the Word of God. Along with faith comes expectation.

▶ Remember that God is a good Father who gives good things to those who ask. He wants to fill you with His joy and fruitfulness.

▶ Get to know Jesus more and more, then you will be able to pray more powerfully in His name, asking according to His purposes and desires, which will always be good toward you.

▶ Give thanks to God when you pray. Jesus said to believe you have received whatever you ask for in prayer. Since you receive it, go ahead and give thanks for it.

▶ Do not waver between faith and doubt. The more you press into God and His Word, the more your doubts will flee and your faith will grow. Then with confidence, you can pray and fully expect to receive what you are asking.

God Works Through Fathers

Believe on the Lord Jesus Christ, and you will be saved,
you and your household.
(Acts 1:31)

God works through fathers. We find a beautiful illustration of this in Acts 16. The story begins with Paul and Silas, when they were thrown in jail at Philippi for preaching the Gospel and setting captives free. Beaten with many stripes, and their feet fastened in stocks, Paul and Silas took this as the perfect opportunity to pray and sing hymns to God. They did not do anything by halves, so everyone in the cell block heard their testimony of praise.

Someone has said that the way *out* is *through*, and that was the case here. As Paul and Silas loudly lifted their hearts to the Lord in prayer and faith, the earth suddenly began to quake. Cell doors came open and shackles began to fall, not just from Paul and Silas, but from every prisoner in the place.

A calamitous thing was happening, at least from the jailer's point of view, for no amount of explaining would ever be sufficient to deliver him from dire consequences. So he drew his sword and was about to kill himself when Paul, seeing this, cried out to him, "Do yourself no harm, for we are all here."

The jailer immediately had a revelation: "This man knows what's going on." He recognized Paul and Silas. He knew why they had been arrested. He had heard them singing and praising God in the middle of the night. And did he not just personally experience the power of God in this very unusual earthquake which loosed all the prisoners?

Now he realized that he needed to know one more thing. So he called for a light, ran to the cell where Paul and Silas had been shackled, and brought them out. Trembling before them, he asked, "Sirs, what must I do to be saved?"

> So they said, "Believe on the Lord Jesus Christ, and you will be saved, you and your household." Then they spoke the word of the Lord to him and to all who were in his house. And he took them the same hour of the night and washed their stripes. And immediately he and all his family were baptized. Now when he had brought them into his house, he set food before them; and he rejoiced, having believed in God with all his household" (Acts 16:31-34)

God works through fathers. On that dark night, deep in the bowels of the Philippian jail, salvation showed up for the jailer, but not just for him only—it showed up for his entire household. As father of the house, he became a gateway for the whole family. Salvation came to them all, not because he was a jailer, but because he was a father.

You see, fathers are conduits for the work of God. That's why honoring parents is on God's Top Ten list. That's why the Fifth Commandment, "Honor your father and your mother," comes with a promise, "that your days may be long upon the land which the LORD your God is giving you" (Exodus 20:12).

God Has Always Worked Through Fathers

God has always worked through fathers. To Adam and Eve, He said, "Be fruitful and multiply; fill the earth and subdue it; have dominion" (Genesis 1:28). This would all come about through fathering. Later, God called out Abram as a father, though he was old and had no children. Nevertheless, God showed him a land and said, "To your descendants I will give this land" (Genesis 12:7). He changed his name to Abraham, which means "Father of Nations." God's reasoning was plain but powerful: "For I have made you a father of many nations" (Genesis 17:5). In Genesis 18:19, God further explained His choice: "For I have known him, in order that he may command his children and his household after him, that they keep the way of the LORD."

Notice that God did not say, "I have known *that* he will command his children," but rather, "I have known him, *in order that* he may command his children." A causality is indicated here, and an intention. The verb "known" is the same verb we find in Genesis 4:1, "Now Adam *knew* Eve and she conceived and bore." It is a term of intimate knowledge and relationship. It brings forth life and purpose.

God said, "I have *known* him." In other words, there was something being fathered in Abraham. Because of that fathering, Abraham would now be able to be a father himself, not merely in the physical, but more importantly, in the spiritual: "That he may command his children and his household after him, that they keep the way of the LORD."

The essence of fatherhood is inheritance, that is, in that which is passed on to the ones who have been fathered. When Moses met God at the burning bush, God revealed Himself in the language of heritage: "I am the God of your father—the God of Abraham, the God of Isaac, and the God of Jacob" (Exodus 3:6).

Moses had not known his father, but there was an inheritance nonetheless, and it reached all the way back to Abraham. What God began in Abraham passed from father to son, from Abraham to Isaac to Jacob, and so on, until it was now Moses' turn. Moses received this inheritance and in so doing received his identity in the world. Fathers are a very important channel for the blessing of God. They help us know who we are and why we are here.

The prophet Elijah also came to understand the importance of fathering. He was a mighty man of God who stirred the Northern kingdom of Israel to a spiritual awakening and performed many miracles. Yet when he was on the run from the wicked Jezebel, he prayed that he might die: "It is enough! Now, Lord, take my life, for I am no better than my fathers!" (1 Kings 19:4). He felt like the end of the line, and truly he was—until God showed him how to instill identity and destiny into someone else. Elijah found Elisha and began fathering him in spiritual things. Thus, he passed the inheritance on to Elisha and in so doing, made it greater.

Fatherhood is such an important matter to God that the very last verse of the Old Testament speaks of another coming of Elijah, to "turn the hearts of the fathers to the children, and the hearts of the children to their fathers" (Malachi 4:6).

The Philippian Father

We do not know the name of the jailer in Philippi. He has always been called, simply, "the Philippian Jailer." But in this day when the curse of fatherlessness is raging in our generation, we ought to begin thinking about this man in a new way. Call him "the Philippian Father." For was that not his greater role? Was that not how he came to fulfill his destiny and, in a measure, transform the world? Yes, it was as a father!

When he cried out in the middle of the night, "What must I do to be saved?" it was a question of eternal significance, no doubt. But the answer he received had even greater import: "Believe on the Lord Jesus Christ, and you will be saved, you *and your household*." You see, it was not just about the jailer himself. God wanted his whole house to come to salvation, to establish in them a new lineage, a flow of blessing that crosses generational boundaries.

In his desperate crying out, this man of Philippi truly became the father he was called to be. Because of him, the Word of God was preached to his family, and salvation came to his entire household. By morning they were all baptized, bearing the mark of God's love upon their lives. And they rejoiced!

More Than Biology

The issue of fatherhood is not limited by biology. You may not be a father in the natural, but you can certainly be a father in the Spirit. You can come into a life-giving relationship with someone else, bearing the incorruptible seed of the Word of God, to impart a legacy of the love of God. Indeed, it is in the spiritual dimension that fatherhood finds its greatest significance.

Fatherhood is not limited by gender, either. All I have said about fathering applies as much to women as to men. A woman can sow seeds of the Spirit and pass on the blessing of God to others just as well as any man can do. No crisis of identity is implied—if a man can learn to take his place as the "bride of Christ," then surely a woman can learn to be a "father" in the Spirit.

Therefore, what I say, I say to all those who will take unto themselves children in whom they can impart the things of God: You are fathers, and when you stand before God, you do not stand merely for yourself, but for your children, your families, and your households. You are an expansive gateway for the blessing, favor and power of God in their lives. The inheritance of God passes through you, for you are fathers, and God works through fathers.

Inheriting Destiny

Psalm 127

A Song of Ascents. Of Solomon.

1   Unless the LORD builds the house,
They labor in vain who build it;
Unless the LORD guards the city,
The watchman stays awake in vain.

2   It is vain for you to rise up early,
To sit up late,
To eat the bread of sorrows;
For so He gives His beloved sleep.

3   Behold, children are a heritage from the LORD,
The fruit of the womb is a reward.

4   Like arrows in the hand of a warrior,
So are the children of one's youth.

5   Happy is the man who has his quiver full of them;
They shall not be ashamed,
But shall speak with their enemies in the gate.

This is a wisdom psalm—it reveals to us the pathway of God's favor. In this case, wisdom compares a way of life that is empty and vain with a life that is fruitful and full of blessing. This psalm was written by Solomon, who was considered the wisest of all men.

It belongs with the Psalms of Ascent (Psalm 120-134), a collection that was used to prepare the heart as one made pilgrimage to Jerusalem each year to celebrate the three big feasts of Israel: Passover, Pentecost and Tabernacles.

Lord, Build Our House

> Unless the LORD builds the house,
> they labor in vain who build it.

This is the first of three vanities Solomon warns us about. The word for "house" comes from the word *banah*, which means "to build." In the natural, we think of a house as a physical structure, an abode made of wood and stone.

But Solomon has something much deeper in mind, so instead of "building," think "family," for a house is a place of relationships. It is a place where inheritances are imparted. Every house bears a name, and that name establishes the family and its inheritance.

Whose name does the house bear? Unless it is name of the LORD, the house is built in vain, and will eventually come to ruin. Only the LORD can build something that will endure. Jesus gives us a vivid description of a house built in vain, and shows us how to build one that endures:

> Whoever hears these sayings of Mine, and does them, I will liken him to a wise man who built his house on the rock; and the rain descended, the floods came, and the winds blew and beat on that house; and it did not fall, for it was founded on the rock.
>
> But everyone who hears these sayings of Mine, and does not do them, will be like a foolish man who built his house on the sand; and the rain descended, the floods came, and the winds blew and beat on that house; and it fell. And great was its fall. (Matthew 7:24-27)

Now, when God builds a house, He is not simply putting together a little social unit—He is planting a seed of hope to reap a harvest that changes the world. It is much more than a dynasty, it is a destiny. The LORD built Abraham a house, and through him blessed all the families of the earth. He built David a house, and through him brought forth a King of Righteousness who reigns forever.

Lord, Guard Our City

Unless the LORD guards the city,
the watchman stays awake in vain.

Just as a house is a place of destiny, so a city is a gathering together of houses for the protection of those destinies. What is more, the destiny of a house sets the destiny of a city. Destroy the house, and the city eventually crumbles.

In the Bible, cities also often served other specific purposes. Some were meant for grain storage, others were destined for treasuries. Solomon had cities specifically designated to accommodate his 40,000 chariots and 12,000 horsemen.

A city must have the purpose of God, but it must also have the protection of God, so Solomon warns us of another vanity. If the Lord is not the one watching over the city, there is no question about whether it will be overcome and brought to nothing. The only question is when. In Isaiah, God tells us of the watch He set for His people:

I have set watchmen on your walls, O Jerusalem;
They shall never hold their peace day or night.
You who make mention of the LORD, do not keep silent,
And give Him no rest till He establishes
And till He makes Jerusalem a praise in the earth.

(Isaiah 62:6-7)

God has set His purposes and given His promises, and He will see them fulfilled. If we look to the LORD to build our house and we obey the watch He has set, crying out to Him continually, holding His promises before Him, and if we do not keep silent, but pursue Him with all our heart, our cities will be places of praise and honor where He is made famous. We will be blessed, and all the earth will be blessed through us.

Lord, Give Us Rest

For so He gives His beloved sleep.

Solomon cautions us about a third vanity. "It is vain to for you to rise us early, to sit up late, to eat the bread of sorrows." Why is it vain? Because the LORD gives His beloved sleep. Or as the New American Standard Bible puts it, "He gives to His beloved even in his sleep."

There is rest in God because it is all about God and not about us. Our provision and protection does not come because of us. It is His doing. The LORD our God does not sleep or slumber, so while we are asleep, He continues to watch over and take care of us. Our part is simply to rest in Him, and that is a matter of faith.

Consider the children of Israel. The generation that wandered around in the wilderness for forty years remained in the desert and died there. The author of Hebrews tells us that, although God had prepared a place of rest for them, "they could not enter in because of unbelief" (Hebrews 3:19).

Think of it. They had the Word of God concerning the wonderful rest He had for them. They had the Gospel preached to them, "but the word which they heard did not profit, not being mixed with faith in those who heard it" (Hebrews 4:2). They had no faith to lay hold of God's Word, so they perished in the wilderness.

The promise for rest, however, still remains. The author of Hebrews tells us that, "we who have believed *do* enter that rest" (Hebrews 4:3).

When the Lord builds our house and watches over our city, we can rest peacefully, knowing that all will be well. Proverbs 3 tells us that when we walk in the wisdom of the Lord we shall enjoy rest. "When you lie down, you will not be afraid. Yes, you will lie down and your sleep will be sweet" (v. 24).

Lord, Give Us Children.

Behold, children are a heritage from the LORD.

And now Solomon has arrived at the central point of his psalm. Everything he has said up to now was simply a preparation for this, and if you miss it, you miss his whole purpose. The clue to how important this is can be found in the word "behold." It is a call to pay close attention, to focus yourself upon, to gaze intently and meditate deeply. When the LORD tells us to "behold," He is directing our attention to a very foundational truth. Just what truth is it, then, that God wants us to give ourselves so wholeheartedly to? Simply this:

Children are a heritage from the LORD!

The word for "children" comes from the word *banah*, the same root word that is used for "build" and "house." The children build up the house; sons and daughters build up the family name.

Children are called a "heritage." That is, they are an inheritance. We receive them from the Lord. He entrusts us with them. Now, inheritances are not given to squander, but to enlarge, and God expects us to treat our inheritance with wisdom, and obey the vision of His purpose.

Adam and Eve were instructed to be fruitful and multiply, to fill the earth and have dominion (Genesis 1:28). What were they to multiply? The image of God, for that is what God created them to be upon the earth. They were to fill the earth with the image of

God and exercise the authority of God. That's the big picture, and as God brings us to redemption through Jesus Christ, we are all called to participate in its fulfillment. So Solomon enlarges the point:

> Like arrows in the hand of a warrior,
>> So are the children of one's youth.

Our job is to receive this great inheritance from the Lord and impart to our children vision, wisdom and direction. We are called to be like warriors, faithfully launching our children as arrows toward their world-changing purpose and destiny in God. There is preparation, as we instruct them in the ways of God, then release, as we send them forth to walk in those ways. So the purpose of God flows from generation to generation. The house is enlarged and its destiny fulfilled.

This is a very blessed and happy state, as Solomon concludes:

> Happy is the man who has his quiver full of them;
>> They shall not be ashamed,
>> But shall speak with their enemies in the gate.

We release our children with the vision and wisdom of God, and the more, the merrier. One shall put a thousand to flight, two shall put ten thousand to flight. They shall not be put to shame but shall overcome all their obstacles.

They shall "speak with their enemies in the gate." The gate of the city is the place of authority and leadership, the place where decisions are made and legal matters are settled. It is also a place of commerce and prosperity. Capture the gates, and you capture city.

The Hebrew word for "speak," *dabar*, literally means to arrange or subdue. As we impart the wisdom and purpose of God to our children, they will subdue their enemies at the gates of the city. There shall be no breaking in or breaking out—only going forth.

Here is where the family and the city come together. The city protects the destiny of the house, the house launches sons and daughters into their destinies, and the sons and daughters prevail at the gate of the city so that it prospers. The inheritance enlarges until the whole earth is filled with the blessing of the LORD.

Lord,

Build our house and create our destiny. Guard our city and protect our destiny. Give us rest and fulfill our destiny. Give us children and pass on to them our destiny.

In Jesus' name, Amen.

Why Jesus Came

*M*any people understand *that* Jesus came into the world. But it is only when you know *why* Jesus came that you can really begin to experience all the blessing He has for you. The following is not a theologically exhaustive list of reasons why He came, but it will help you get started on a new life with Him.

Jesus Came to do the Father's Will

> I have come down from heaven, not to do My own will, but the will of Him who sent Me. (John 6:38)

> For I seek not to please Myself but Him who sent Me. (John 5:30)

Jesus was perfectly in tune with the heart of the Father, and delighted in doing His will. His ministry was thoroughly guided by it, for He said, "The Son can do nothing by Himself; He can do only what He sees His Father doing, because whatever the Father does the Son does also" (John 5:19). "Whatever I say is just what the Father has told me to say" (John 12:50).

Jesus never took it upon Himself to say or do anything except what the Father told Him to say and do. This was the pattern for His ministry. Everything He did perfectly expressed the will of God. Even on His final night in the Garden of Gethsemane, He prayed, "Nevertheless not my will, but Yours, be done" (Luke 22:42).

Jesus Came to Serve and to Give His Life

As Jesus' ministry on earth was drawing to a close, He spoke to the disciples about true greatness: "You know that those who are considered rulers over the Gentiles lord it over them, and their great ones exercise authority over them. Yet it shall not be so among you; but whoever desires to become great among you shall be your servant. And whoever of you desires to be first shall be slave of all" (Mark 10:42-44).

In the world, greatness is measured by how much weight you can throw around, or how many people you can order about, or how much rank you can pull. But Jesus turned that on its head. The great ones are not those who know how to "lord it" over others, but those who know how to become the servant—the slave!—of all. This kind of servanthood is not so we can one day become great leaders and put aside the role of being a servant. Quite the contrary, this kind of servanthood exactly defines what a great leader is—the servant of all. "For even the Son of Man did not come to be served, but to serve, and to give His life a ransom for many" (Mark 10:45).

It is the very nature of Jesus to give and to serve, for Jesus is truly God. God is love (1 John 4:8), and it is the very nature of love to give. "For God so loved the world that He gave His only begotten Son" (John 3:16).

In doing the Father's will, Jesus demonstrated the Father's love, giving His own life as a ransom for us—paying a terrible price He did not owe in order to redeem us from a debt we could never pay.

Jesus Came to Seek and to Save

The Son of Man did not come to destroy men's lives but to save them. (Luke 9:56)

For the Son of Man has come to seek and to save that which was lost. (Luke 19:10)

Jesus did not come to destroy us, but to save us. That is the promise of the Christmas story. For the angel of the Lord said to Joseph, "Do not be afraid to take to you Mary your wife, for that which is conceived in her is of the Holy Spirit. And she will bring forth a Son, and you shall call His name Jesus, for He will save His people from their sins" (Matthew 1:20-21).

The very name of Jesus, in its Hebrew form, *Yeshua*, means "Yahweh saves!" It comes from the Hebrew *yasha*, which means to rescue or remove someone from burden, oppression or danger.

Jesus Came to Destroy the Works of the devil

> For this purpose the Son of God was manifested, that He might destroy the works of the devil. (1 John 3:8)

Jesus did not come to destroy our lives, but to destroy the bondage which has plagued life ever since Adam and Eve, when the devil first led mankind into sin. But even then, the Lord made a promise about One who would come and destroy the devil and his works. He said to the serpent, "I will put enmity between you and the woman, and between your seed and her Seed [Jesus]; He shall bruise your head, and you shall bruise His heel" (Genesis 3:15). In theological terms, this is called the *protoevangelium*, the first mention of the Gospel recorded in Scripture.

The devil tried to destroy the people of God from Adam to Abraham, but he could not. He tried to destroy the descendents of Abraham, the children of Israel, but he could not. He tried to destroy the lineage of Jesus in every generation, but he could not. He tried to destroy the ministry of Jesus in the wilderness temptation, but he could not. Finally, he tried to destroy the lifework of Jesus by nailing him to the cross, little realizing that it was for this reason that Jesus came: to give His life on the cross as a ransom for many.

The devil could never destroy the plans and purposes of God, not even if he had all eternity to try. But through the Cross and the empty tomb, Jesus destroyed all the works of the devil. Sin, sickness, poverty, strife, death and everything that stands against the people of God—all the power of the devil has been broken, including fear and death.

> Inasmuch then as the children have partaken of flesh and blood, He Himself likewise shared in the same, that through death He might destroy him who had the power of death, that is, the devil, and release those who through fear of death were all their lifetime subject to bondage. (Hebrews 2:14-15)

Jesus is now seated at the right hand of the Father, "far above all principality and power and might and dominion, and every name that is named" (Ephesians 1:21).

Jesus Came That We Might Have Life More Abundantly

> The thief does not come except to steal, and to kill, and to destroy. I have come that they may might have life, and that they may have it more abundantly. (John 10.10)

The thief is the one who tries to deceive God's people, seeking to turn them away from God's purposes. He comes to steal, kill and destroy. These are the works of the devil, but Jesus came to destroy all those works.

Jesus came that we might have life, and have it more abundantly. Our God is a God of abundance. His paths drip abundance (Psalm 65:11). He is able "to do exceedingly abundantly above all we ask or think according to the power that works in us" (Ephesians 3:20) and He is able "to make all grace abound toward you, that you, always having all sufficiency in all things, may have abundance for every good work" (2 Corinthians 9:8). He gives to us out of His abundance so that we can give to others out of our abundance, and so share in His ministry.

Jesus Came to Proclaim the Favor of the Lord

> The Spirit of the LORD is upon Me, because He has anointed Me to preach the gospel to the poor. He has sent Me to heal the broken-hearted, to proclaim liberty to the captives and recovery of sight to the blind, to set at liberty those who are oppressed; to proclaim the acceptable year of the LORD. (Luke 4:18-19)

Jesus began His preaching ministry with this passage, which comes from Isaiah 61:1-2. This wonderful text is the charter of Jesus' ministry, for after reading it, He said, "Today this Scripture is fulfilled in your hearing" (Luke 4:21). In it, we find that Jesus came to preach, to heal and to deliver the captives—in short, to proclaim the favor of the Lord.

Throughout the rest of this chapter, indeed, throughout the rest of the Gospel of Luke, and in the other Gospels as well, we find Jesus preaching, healing and casting out demons. We also see Him choosing the disciples "that they might be with Him, and that He might send them out to preach, and to have power to heal sickness and to cast out demons" (Mark 3:14-15). Then we see Him actually sending them out to do just that (Mark 6:7-13).

Before His ascension into heaven, we see Jesus commissioning the disciples with these words: "All authority has been given to Me in heaven and on earth. Go therefore and make disciples of all the nations, baptizing them ... teaching them to observe all things that I have commanded" (Matthew 28:18-20)." The disciples were not only to continue these charter works, but they were to disciple others in them, as well. "Go into all the world and preach the gospel to every creature ... And these signs will follow those who believe: In My name they will cast out demons ... they will lay hands on the sick, and they will recover" (Mark 16:15-18). Their commission is our commission, too, for it is in this same way that we are to proclaim that the time of God's favor has come.

Jesus Came for You

God so loved the world that He gave His only begotten Son, that whoever believes in Him should not perish but have everlasting life. (John 3:16)

If you are a "whoever," Jesus came for you. He came to reconcile you to the heart of the Father and to give His life as a ransom for you. He came to seek you out and save you from sin. He came to destroy all the works of the devil in your life and replace them with the wonderful abundance of His own life. He came to forgive your sins, heal your sicknesses, and proclaim that the time of God's favor toward you has come.

We receive all these things by faith—taking God at His Word. The promise is that "whoever believes in Him should not perish but have everlasting life." The Bible says,

If you confess with your mouth the Lord Jesus and believe in your heart that God has raised Him from the dead, you will be saved. For with the heart one believes unto righteousness, and with the mouth confession is made unto salvation. For the Scripture says, "Whoever believes on Him will not be put to same." (Romans 10:9-11)

If you have never received the Lord Jesus Christ before, you can do it right now. Simply say a little prayer to the Father. It doesn't have to be a fancy prayer; just speak to Him from your heart. Tell Him that you believe His promises and ask the Lord Jesus Christ to be your Savior. Then new life will begin for you.

Dear Lord,

I confess that I am a sinner and that I have come short of your glory. But I believe that You love me and that Jesus died on the Cross for my sins. I confess with my mouth that Jesus is Lord, and I believe in my heart that You have raised Him from the dead. I now receive Your wonderful gift of salvation through Jesus Christ my Lord, and I ask You to give me Your Holy Spirit, as You have promised.

In Jesus' name, Amen.

Also from Walking Barefoot Ministries

Walking Barefoot
Living in Prayer, Faith & the Power of God
by Jeff Doles
ISBN 0-9744748-0-0

Drawn from the story of Moses at the burning bush, *Walking Barefoot* speaks of an ongoing relationship, a partnership with God in the world. It is about learning to walk with Him, flowing in His power to fulfill His purposes. In this book by you will learn about the power of faith and how to activate it, the power of praying God's will and speaking God's Word, the power of agreement, the power of praying over your children, the power of Jesus' healing ministry today ... and much more.

Praying With Fire
Learning to Pray With Apostolic Power
by Jeff Doles
ISBN 0-9744748-6-X

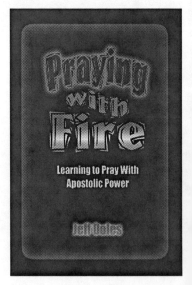

Discover the principles that made the apostles so effective in their prayer life: a heart perfected in love, a habit of devotion, a deep confidence in God and His Word, and a reliance upon the Holy Spirit. You will also learn how to pray the prayers they prayed —powerful prayers that express the heart of God ... eight ground-breaking evangelistic prayers, ten pastoral prayers, fourteen prayers of blessing, fifteen prayers of thanksgiving and thirteen glory-filled doxologies.

Also from **Walking Barefoot Ministries**

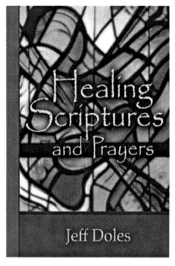

Healing Scriptures and Prayers

by Jeff Doles

ISBN 0-9744748-1-9

God wants you well!

The Word of God frequently reveals God's great desire to bless and heal His people. Healing Scriptures and Prayers is designed to help you lay hold of God's willingness and receive your healing—spirit, soul and body.

also

**Healing Scriptures and Prayers
(read by Jeff Doles)**

Sit back and relax while these Scriptures, read by Jeff Doles, wash over you and stir up your faith to receive God's healing promises. The prayers on these CDs will help you exercise your faith as you present God's Word before Him with joy and expectation. The gentle background music will refresh you as you meditate on the healing Word of God. Adapted from our book, these recordings are great for soaking prayer!

CD 1: Old Testament Scriptures
CD 2: New Testament Scriptures
CD 3: The Healing Names of God
CD 4: The Healing Ministry of Jesus

P 123

CPSIA information can be obtained at www.ICGtesting.com
Printed in the USA
LVOW040309190113

316391LV00001B/464/A